MYSTICAL
Scotland

MYSTICAL
Scotland

ANN LINDSAY MITCHELL

with drawings by her son
DUNCAN BRADLEY

British Library Cataloguing in Publication Data
Mitchell, Ann Lindsay
Mystical Scotland
I. Title
941.1

ISBN 1 85877 005 X

Typeset by XL Publishing Services, Nairn
Printed in Great Britain
By J.W. Arrowsmith, Bristol,
For Thomas & Lochar
PO Box 4, Nairn IV12 4HU

Contents

Introduction

Mystical Scotland is a land of kelpies and curses, spiritual stones and ancient rocks with pagan overtones. Mystical Scotland contains deep-rooted religious beliefs often perceived to be as harsh as the Scottish climate, as well as a strange mixture of self mockery and confident, even brash self worth through education and enterprise. The Scots have the popular image of being dour and canny, but are in fact a nation resounding with music and drama and laughter. Capable of the grand gesture to be sure – even our swaggering national costume reflects this – but also cautious to the point of ridicule.

Why does Scotland and its people radiate such contrasting enigmas? Why does the Scottish character also emit such stereo-typed and to my mind untruthful images?

I began this book by casting around for the less obvious background to the image of Scotland, attempting to sweep aside the common clichés. My search has taken me into little-charted depths of history; the unexpected, little-known. Not the sort of usual tales read by children in their history lessons, or tourists in guide books.

What has led to the images of the Scots character? From what colourful and eventful ages past has the Scots character gained least or most? How much have the Scots retained the influences of their past? How much has the geographical lie of the land, the volatile climate and the extravagantly contrasting landscape contributed to their character?

Mystical Scotland searches behind the common images to unearth these roots, because while it may be a land encompassing soft, rich, productive farmlands, and thinly covered acres of granite mountain, a land with an unfair amount of heart-stopping beauty, it is above all a land which has produced an intriguing race of people, and it is surely these Scots folk who are the ultimate mystery of all.

The Scots people are unique. All over the world to be a Scot is an accepted diplomatic entrée into local society – a passport not given so freely to our British neighbours. How on earth have the Scots managed to walk this tightrope? Why do we still exude a sense of national background? Why, in short, are the Scots such an individualistic, opportunistic race, volatile and pugnacious and so very different from our British neighbours?

The Scottish national flag says so much to me. Flamboyantly adorned with a scarlet lion rampant on an acidic yellow background, I have so often wondered why. Why do we have such an obviously foreign animal flying over our heads, and coloured in such hard tones, when our landscape is the epitome of muted, understated colours?

The fighting lion rampant not only adorns this national flag, but also appears in many of the clan badges. The hills and mountains of the Scottish highlands would have thundered to the roars of many varieties of feared animals now extinct. But lions were never an indigenous species here. Yes, there were wolves, eagles and wild boars, all fiercely hunted and immortalised in many of the heraldic symbols of Scottish clans.

Nearly all clan emblems pay scant regard to the softer, church based images. Punched into these emblems are snarling wolves and hunting dogs, heavily tusked wild boars at bay, and innumerable chopped off heads of imaginative, but improbable wild beasts.

Wild wolves, wolf winds, hunted wolves, all play their part in our primitive culture, which lives on today at each Highland Games, pinned onto woolly Glengarries. Heraldic flags and costumes are very much part of our lives.

Fearsome acts of bravery may have been enacted in the pursuit of survival, now commemorated in clan badges, and welded together in battling for a common cause, the Scots soldiers gained an awesome reputation. 'A Highlander never retreats' surprised many a chastened enemy. The vivid imagery of the lion rampant can only be an extension of character which is overtly brave and courageous, and a touch pugnacious.

The pitting of man versus wolves and wild boars may be long gone. Guns may have taken over in organised slaughtering rituals, when man is in no danger except from his own stupidity, but search deeply and you will find that still today on these shores is enacted a hunting expedition of probably medieval origins and style. The hunting of the guga – a seabird – encompasses all the elements of bravery, mixed emotions and understated drama. It is a rite of passage which is not deliberately kept secret, but equally deliberately un-publicised. It is a link with a hunting past in which may lie an example of our forbears way of life. It gives us but a blinking glimpse into a basic past, and an understanding of how the harsh seas and way of surviving have been so influential.

Mixed in with the hunting past and struggle for survival goes romance. Who can point an accurate finger at the widespread source for a dour reputation? I can point firmly at a jolly race, full of endless excuses for celebration.

The Scots are a race with a huge capacity for enjoyment. There are all those blood stirring tunes from bagpipes. Anyone who has listened all day to the skirl of pipes at a Highland Games will have the sounds reverberating in their ears for hours, rather like the echoes of the sea. There is also hauntingly beautiful music from Scots fiddlers. Both instruments are the mainstay of innumerable local events.

Again, unlike our near neighbours, Scots celebrations are less of a national organised event, much more an ingrained, very personal feature of everyday life. Highland Games are a reminder of merry gatherings which were primarily for the participation of local folk. Scotland is the nation which spawned the tryst, realigning the true meaning of the event, which was in reality a commercial cattle market, into the imagery of a romantic meeting place.

The meaning of the word tryst became associated less with the drovers and their cattle – although that indeed is now a pastoral odyssey in misty memory – than as a lyrical romantic and private meeting between lovers. So to the hard commercial world of the great cattle trysts of the 18th century. The wild Highlanders led their beasts down to the nearest points in the Lowlands as their suspicious nature would allow. These trysts became a magnet for the bards, songsters and musicians, who would provide the romantic backdrop for those travellers.

And music, romance and enjoyment are all brought together by the fame of the Scots wedding. The details of rural weddings have been recorded by astonished early travellers as well as closely observed by disapproving country ministers.

Much of a Scots wedding is taken up with sheer exuberance, of which dancing was, and continues to be a major feature. Lost wedding dances are almost too many to document, but kissing dances, rigadoon-a-daisy dances and fairy dances must surely encompass all the depth of a romantic soul.

Also woven into the happy personality of Scottish character were the colourful, nomadic 'travellers'. These were a unique collection of personalities who had banded together and formed their very own culture. They consisted of a raggle taggle group whose ancestors allegedly had left the field of Culloden, too ashamed to return home, as well as those misfits of society whose desire was to roam the countryside. They were not descended from the true Romanies, but formed a culture and language all of their own. To this wandering way of life they added some charmed customs. Marriage and music were elevated by these free spirits. Before the red tapes of bureaucracy tightened its noose round their way of life, weddings were clinched on a remote road in Argyll, with the happy couple standing upon a stone heart, roughly embedded in the road with convenient round stones.

Their methods of earning a living also had an aura of secrecy. To these folk alone was known the whereabouts of the famous, elusive Scottish river pearl. To this day, fishing for these pearls is done by itinerant, carefree folk of the road. They alone know the secrets of where to scoop up the rich pearls, as they have done in the same way since medieval times, handing down the locations only by word of mouth.

To see these fishermen in action today is a near impossible task. The Scots have a long tradition of being able to vanish before even the most determined eyes. And it is not only in the eyes of those travellers that strange beliefs and secrets have been handed down, unwritten through many generations.

The Lee Penny, immortalised by Sir Walter Scott in his book *Talisman*, still sits in the noble house in which it has rested since the days of the Crusades, and the educated owners still believe in the properties of curing with which this unprepossessing little stone is said to be imbued.

The Scots mingling of the accepted religious beliefs and the misty magical world which existed before St Columba landed on Scottish shores is an undercurrent which darts through many Scots customs. The same generation, while secretly keeping alive the pre-Christian customs in their homes, would also defy a landlord who unwisely tried to impose his own brand of religious beliefs on his subjects. This defiance was staggering in its actions. Whole congregations hired boats, moored just outside the jurisdiction of the law, or worshipped outdoors rather than under an unwelcome roof. But at the same time, members of this same congregation would accord a new born baby with magical protective tweaks of scarlet thread or twigs of local rowans for extra insurance. Should a fragile baby die unbaptised though, it would be buried outside the churchyard, and if possible upon a gentle hill, from where the fairies could pluck the child's spirit that much the easier.

But Scottish religious beliefs are deep-rooted, and to the outsider have produced an army of deeply committed men whose lives were usually a curious mixture of intense devotion to their God, with a no nonsense practicality. From St Columba to Lord Macleod of Fuinery, who founded and rebuilt a place of worship on Iona centuries apart, this thread of religious belief runs ever strong.

To these shores came religious men who have gone down in the Scots history books as saints. To the puzzled visitor of today, their predilection for casting themselves away on the most inhospitable lumps of island rock explains something of their sheer courage. They also set standards of ruggedness, self deprivation and formidable beliefs which have lasted for generations.

Travelling through Scotland, you come across a lonely church abruptly set down miles from habitation, but which would have at one time been at a crossroads for hamlets now lost or out of sight. Also, there are tiny churches situated as though cast away on the edges of island beaches, keeping a sea eagle's eye over water which claimed so many lives with its unpredictable tide rips, sudden squalls, or whispering sea monsters and enchanted sea fairies. To their doors came generations whose livelihood depended on defying elements both real and imaginary, and whose worshippers prayed openly to a God, as well as secretly for deliverance from un-God like wraiths. To doubly ensure their survival at sea, sailors would also place their faith in the value of money. In the far northern isles, hard currency would be handed over to an elderly lady who 'sold' winds, while on the Clyde, walking round a stone called Granny Kempoch settled nerves before setting sail.

Their descendants have demonstrated much of the same indomitable character but firmly within the mainstream of life. The 'heather priests' of the west coast of Scotland have few monuments to their itinerant way of life. Their paths are little known if at all, as they trampled the hills from one remote rural community to another, staying as long as they were needed and wandering off again to minister to the next hamlet when duty was done, having demanded little in the way of reward, apart from thanks, a rough bed for the night and sustenance largely based on oatmeal.

Oatmeal played a major role in the lives of all Scots, and even has a day in the year named 'meal Monday'. To better himself, a young Scot from whatever background had a head start in the acquisition of advanced education, hundreds of years before many of his contemporaries in Europe. To University he would stride, also carrying his 'peck' of oatmeal, which would be swung off his shoulders onto the grateful floor of a landlady, as part of his keep. 'Meal Monday' was midway through the term, when he would return home to replenish his supplies.

In the curious mixture that forged the Scots character, when Scot would fight Scot to the death over a clan dispute, or in support of an unknown King from across the seas, the Scots were united in their willingness to place education above all.

When St Andrews University opened its doors in 1412, students trooped on foot from far afield. Quick to follow suit in this path to learning, Scotland could boast four Universities, to England's mere two, Oxford and Cambridge.

Why did the Scots place such store in the availability of learning for all? The ancestors of these young Scots came from an impressive mingling of blood. Fearsome Nordic invaders, probably the cream of their land in terms of courage and navigational knowledge, settled down eventually with Celtic immigrants from Ireland, bringing with them the artistic brilliance which stamped its mark on decoration in the great monastic cultures. Other remnants of races drifted onto Scottish shores. Roman legionnaires stayed behind, Spanish sailors were effectively abandoned when shipwrecked. As today, they were too few in number to form a national ghetto, and so were absorbed into the Scots race.

To these shores too came by accident or stealth artistic influences which were then quickly claimed as Scottish. Tartan could have had a French ancestor, the Paisley pattern from the symbol of life in Asia, and the Fair Isle pattern from the Baltics.

Then there was the uncertain climate. Great swathes of glen and mountain would be shrouded in mists and rain, clearing with spectacular speed, to reveal rainbows and sun, then just as rapidly vanish. Sometimes the earth would be clamped with frost and snow, other times the sun would parch the earth for a month. Contending with such a climate, little wonder that the inhabitants cast around for a life which might offer an escape route, a path to understanding, and an opportunity to use that brain which had been tuned by generations of imaginative story tellers.

From glens they came to seats of learning, leaving behind a culture which not only prayed generously to a Christian God, but also, for good measure, cast a canny Scots eye towards ancient pagan festivals, such as Beltane, Hallows Een, and much swinging of flaming torches and lighting of bonfires. To appease the gods, and in order to ensure the best weather prospects for the coming crops was well worth defying the local man of the church.

In living memory, many rituals were enacted to ensure a generous harvest.

Away in the hills, far from prying eyes, there was, and probably still is, the Cailleach family. They are a 'family' of stones, carefully placed in their 'house' up in the hills for the summer, to ensure good weather. The great festival of Halloween may live on today, and is familiar to all, but the festival of Beltane, which took place at the beginning of May, was to celebrate and encourage the commencement of summer. The celebrations centred on an elaborate ritual of lighting fires, when a great blaze was kindled and then from its flames, a blazing torch was carried to each house. Within the hearth, the old fire had been extinguished, and the new fire was kindled.

It was a festival of brilliance, with fire and the colour yellow much in evidence. Also part of this celebration were Beltane bannocks, and special custard, laughing, dancing and happiness looking forward to warmer days. How curious then, that this uncomplicated celebration has died, while others of equal pre-Christian and ancient origin are still alive. But at least the Beltane is well entrenched in modern times, as Tullybelton, an area in which this ritual was practised, exists four miles north of Perth.

For a small country, Scotland has a heady mixture of different cultures, customs and climates of opinion. For centuries Scot fought Scot, although at that time, they were not of course lumped together under one name. In the Lowlands, they fought the Romans, and for good measure anyone else unwise enough to stray over from south of the border. They also fought each other, usually over cattle and the riches of the land. Amid the islands, the clans too fought each other. Sometimes it was for land, as the winner would rename himself with that most romantic of titles, the Lord of the Isles. But battles were also fought over principles. There were rights and wrongs, snatching of wives and daughters, and their retrieval, slanging matches which had to be avenged, and curses which required a slaughter of the perpetrator. Pride and honour were of equal importance as jurisdiction of the strategic sea channel routes. The west coast lords were just that, Lords of the Isles.

On the east coast, land was of paramount importance, and huge tracts of Scotland were amassed by the great families of Forbes, Farquharson, Gordon, and Ogilvy. Their survival as feudal overlords also depended on allegiance from all, and usurpers were ruthlessly demolished. In addition to their desire for land ownership with all the wealth the north east farming lands could produce, came worry about their succession. Carefully organised marriages ensured an even greater spread of wealth, and the direct succession via sons was much cherished. Family curses upon many of these acquisitive overlords were strangely effective, even more so, as they have leaked even into the present generations.

Today, the people fall into as widely differing beliefs, both political and religious, and attitudes are as strongly voiced as in times past. Perhaps it is the lingering on of a national character based on pride and honour on the one side, and hard nosed acquisition and commerce on the other, which begins to make sense of the Scots character.

But if all this sounds far too serious, then to this mixture I must also add an endearing ability to laugh at themselves, – read *Scotland the What?* – , and a higgeldy piggeldy line of eccentricity.

Great tomes have filled the library shelves about the genealogy of the 'great houses' of Scotland, the names ringing like military battalions, the Gordons, Argylls, Seaforths and Sutherlands. But who knows about the reverse side to this serious side? The Earl of Bute getting himself thoroughly immersed in the search for spiritualism and the 'second sight' – and with an American spinster of dubious character, come to that. Then there was the Duke of Atholl who nearly upgraded his rank to King of Albania, and this all happened here, in Scotland, in the 20th century. But finally, there is the King of the Picts, alive and well at the time of writing, and established in his own separate kingdom on Skye, to the intense irritation of the local civil servants.

Royal connections have kept much of the tourist industry alive and kicking in Scotland, as we are a nation whose desire for a King seems unlikely to wane. Many Scots nurture the image of Royalty, with a devoted following still poking around the history books to track down the true claimant to the Stuart throne. Within a country which still harbours such thoughts, there is nowhere more steadfast than the ideals of some of the great old families in the land. At Traquair, an ancient house near Peebles, where once William the Lion held court, holds fast to the tradition that the great main gates will remain closed until a Stuart once again reigns.

Within Mystical Scotland are many unexpected facets of the Scots land, culture and character. From times long long past to the present day, the mysticism of Scotland is sometimes slightly unravelled, but mostly lives on.

Great Gugas,
Giant Snakes
Werewolves,
Wolf Winds,
Elf Shot,
Elephants
and 'Beaveris'
Tales.

THE ROARS AND ECHOES OF THE SCOTTISH WILDERNESS

It was a mere few hundred years ago – but a blip on the age of a land which, on the rocky land north west is one of the oldest in Europe – that the Scottish countryside would have echoed and shuddered to the roar of many animals which have now passed into memory and folklore.

The elk or moose (*Alces alces*) roamed free until around AD 1300. The fearsome wild boar (*Sus scrofa*) would have rampaged and scuffled and snuffled under one of the many thousands of oak trees. And, surprisingly, the beaver (*Castor fiber*) was mentioned by Hector Boece, and found in the Highlands until the 15th or 16th century, being hunted for its skin. An Act of Parliament from the reign of David I records 'beaveris skins' among Scottish exports.

Hector Boece, who lived from around 1465 until 1536, was a native of Dundee who eventually became the first principal of the newly founded King's College, in the University of Aberdeen. In his book on the 'History of Scotland', written in Latin, he offers tantalising glimpses of life at the time. He makes but a passing reference to beavers skins, giving rise to speculation that such animals and their skins were too common for much recording. But widespread might well have been the gnawing and dam building of beavers in a land with a plentiful supply of trees and fresh water. On elderly maps just to the east of Blairgowrie is marked a 'Beavershire'. Who knows how many other places were named after their animal occupants?

Brown bears (*Ursus artos*) roamed free in Scotland until around the 9th or 10th centuries, almost certainly fiercely hunted to extinction by man.

Hunting of these animals was probably mostly done by men in small numbers, and mainly by stalking and stealth, but other methods might well have been used. The Inverness Scientific Society of 1884 examined some evidence of hunting in one of their expeditions in 1884, and conjectured as to the methods used:

'about half a mile beyond the Tower of Culloden, on the road to Nairnside, they halted for purpose of examining a low stone-way, or zigzag dyke, running with breaks for a distance of about eight or ten miles, from Croy to Duntelchaig. Mr Ross said various explanations were given for the riding of this series of dykes. One is that they formed a division or fence to prevent the cattle of the tribes of Strathnairn from mixing with those of the valley of the Ness. Another, and one which commended itself most to him, was that they were hunting dykes or traps. This was also the popular belief of the older people of the district, which seemed to lend some force to the explanation. The wild beasts, Mr Ross said, were hunted or driven till they reached the wall, along which they ran till a turn of the dyke enclosed them in a cul-de-sac, like a stake net, and so being hemmed in by the hunters were captured. Mr Fraser, whose attention he had directed to the matter, expressed the opinion that the stones were only the basis of a wooden palisade. The walls seldom extend over half a mile in length in any one place, and are placed at irregular intervals. The general opinion of those present was that the dykes had been built and used for hunting purposes; and that this peculiar mode of construction was followed with the view of trapping the animals in the manner Mr Ross has described.'

Near the Cairn O Mount, from the road to Fettercairn over to Banchory, other walls can be discerned, and similar conclusions were drawn about the use of these walls for driving animals into a trap, but there is not conclusive evidence as to the exact use of these walls; their history does seem to be lost in time.

But the one animal which has kindled much mysticism, hatred, maligning and plain fear was plentiful until only a couple of centuries ago.

Proudly roaming the great wooded glens of Scotland, and relentlessly killed by man until the 18th century, was the wolf. There are a selection of stories as to where the last of this persecuted pack was formally killed. One of the most persistent legends attributes this deed to a MacQueen, from the lands of Mackintosh of Mackintosh, Invernesshire, in 1743.

That the wolf was widespread in the Highlands there is little doubt. Wolves howling on the Highland wind would have daunted many a traveller, and they were feared sufficiently for rest houses or 'spittals' to be built. The bold traveller would progress only as far as a spittal before nightfall. But more feared than the wolf by day and when alive – and there is doubt upon the truth of marauding packs of hungry man-eating wolves – the equally profound fear was of wolves when dead.

To save the corpse from the horror of being eaten by wolves, people went to Herculean efforts to ensure that their deceased loved ones were safe over the water.

Islands such as Handa off Sutherland, Tanera in North West Ross, Inishail on Loch Awe and Eilean Munde on Loch Leven, Argyll became the safe resting place of many local inhabitants. No wolf would brave the width of water to reach such a haven.

But although the wolf joined the ranks of the extinct, along with other occupiers of ancient Scotland, the fear, superstition and cult of the wolf was alive well before this happened and survived in the body of the werewolf.

That collector of folklore, King James VI, wrote in his *Daemonlogie*, (written before 1597) questioning some of the nature of spirits generally;

'And are not our war woolfes one sort of these spirits also, that haunts and troubles some houses and dwelling places?'

The cult of the werewolf was based to some extent on a belief widespread in Europe of men putting on a wolf skin and assuming magical properties, much in the same way as the deep belief in witchlike women who would sneak ashore in seal skins and steal children or entice men to their watery graves.

Right across the social spectrum, there was a wolfish tremor. Insults were hurled via wolves.

In the records of the Presbytery of Kelso of 6 November 1660, a memorial is noted that 'Mitchell Usher, or Wishart at Sprouston and Mausie Ker, his wife complean of John Brown, weaver ther, for calling him a werewolf, and her a witch.

A gypsy curse which enacted a terrible price was put on the Earl of Lindsay and his wife by the mother of two dumb lads caught poaching, and subsequently put to death by the Earl.

'By all the demons of hell, I curse you! For you, Lady Crawford, you shall not see the sun set; you and the unborn babe you carry will both be buried in the same grave; and for you Lord Crawford, you shall die a death that would make the boldest man ever born of woman, even to witness, shriek with fear.'

Lady Crawford died that evening, and her husband was supposedly torn asunder by wolves, they being the spirits of the two dumb brothers.

Also, up the social pecking order it was thought useful to incorporate such a fearsome animal into the family annals.

Basil Spence, writing many years ago in the *Scots Magazine*, remarks on at least one Scottish coat of arms. On the front of an ancient building in Edinburgh's Cowgate, known as the 'French Ambassadors Chapel', the head of the 'war woolf' was sculpted with the legend *Speravi et Inveni*.

Nisbet, an old Scottish heraldic writer described this animal carving as containing:

'a body like a wolf, having four feet with long toes and a tail; it is headed like a man – called in our books a warwolf passant – and three stars in chief argent; which are also to be seen cut upon a stone above an old entry of a house in the Cowgate in Edinburgh above the foot of Libberton's Wynd which belonged formerly to the name of Dickieson, which seems to be from the Dickstons, by the stars with which they carry.'

This pediment was apparently removed to Drumsheugh House, but has now vanished.

Allusions to the wolf are preserved in personal and tribal names. For instance Cinel Loarirn, or modern Lorn in Argyll might well be derived from the Gaelic Loarn, or wolf.

And the great lady of Highland legend Cailleach Bheur was supposedly mistress of the wolves as well of the deer, which she drove around in herds. She was credited with the ability to control the 'wolf winds', perhaps named because of their ferocity or occurrence in the time of year when the wolves, whilst roaming the moors and forests became bolder, hungrier, more frightening and aggressive.

Even in the present day, a fierce wolf wind would be an apt term for the worst of winter gales.

THE WILD DEVIL CAT

The Scottish wildcat has also given rise to many exaggerated stories and has acquired a mythical status all of its own.

At the tip of Glen Lyon in Perthshire, there is the Clach Tagnairn nan Cat, or the Stone of the Devil Cat.

Every Hallowe'en, a ferocious wildcat, black all over and bigger than the usual type, arrived and took up proud stance on the stone. Other wildcats would surround this stone, and sit in a circle round about, welcoming this intruder.

In 1838 a traveller stumbled upon this event, and was instantly attacked by the gang of cats. Just managing to throw them off, he escaped, and staggered on his way to the nearby Woodend House, where he was offered help by the occupants, shocked to find a dead wildcat clinging to his back.

ELF SHOT

The death of cattle for some unexplained reason was, even until the turn of the century, popularly attributed to the fairies or elves.

W. Hunter, writing in *Biggar and the House of Fleming* published in 1862 declared that such animals which just fell down dead quite suddenly had, of course, been the target of elf shot, a belief to which was added credence by the finding from time to time of flint arrowheads in the ground.

From the annals of the Banff Field Club of 1887, it is recorded that:

'I remember hearing an old farmer, long ago dead, when one of his cattle had died on the hill, from what I take to have been some sudden disease of the heart and lungs, conjecting, among other casualties that may have happened to it, that perhaps it was shot-o-deid. He said that it was the work of fairies and that the flint arm heads were the weapons used by them for the purpose.'

This shooting by magical means was called 'shute-a-dead', an expression used countrywide even when the cause was not necessarily mysterious and to shute a dead was also to die; a phrase used when people are very ill with any disease.

Even Robbie Burns immortalised the deed in *Tam O' Shanter*:

'For mony a beast to dead she shot
And perish'd mony a bonnie boat'.

HUNTING THE GUGA

The men set out quietly one day in late summer, crossing over the unpredictable sea from Port of Ness on Lewis to arrive at one of the least accessible and uninviting lumps of rock around Britain.

The island of Sula Sgeir is little more than a giant boulder of rock jutting out from the Atlantic. To find this speck on a map, draw a line from the northernmost tip of Lewis, known as the Butt of Lewis, to the northwestern tip of the mainland, at Cape Wrath. By drawing imaginary lines into a triangle, going northwards, there is Sula Sgeir.

There is no topsoil and no vegetation. It is so remote and inhospitable that no-one inhabits this lump or has done so in the past, with the single, and possibly only exception of Bruinhilda, who arrived at the beginning of the 12th century. She was the sister of St Ronan, and is thought to have built a monastic cell here.

The Island of Lewis is rich in its collection of prehistoric stones, such as cairns, brochs and forts, as well as the famous standing stones of Callanish. Certainly monastic cells were set up by several early Christian settlers, who chose isolated places not only for their safety, but also to enjoy solitude. Their choice was frequently focused on appallingly desolate places.

Sula Sgeir certainly fits the bill. One area is known as the Chapel Promontory, where there is a 'beehive' construction believed to be the remains of Bruinhilda's cell. These 'beehive' cells were built with flat stones, which would have been the only building materials available on islands such as this, and remains of this type of shelter are to be seen all over the outer isles. What marks out Sula Sgeir from so many other places is the total lack of natural fresh water and vegetation. Moreover, there is virtually no safe landing place, as the rock descends almost vertically into the sea. A tiny entrance with a cave sheltered from the prevailing southwest winds is the sole method of approach for landing. This cave bisects the island.

To this rocky outcrop come sea birds in their thousands, if not hundreds of thousands. And so to this island, from time immemorial, men have come risking their lives to catch and kill these young birds. They came for reasons of survival. The meat from the sea birds was greatly prized as a change from a purely fish diet, and islanders followed a yearly tradition of a small select band of their folk casting off from home to catch as many as the community needed to supplement their food over the winter. It was a dangerous undertaking. They would risk much in the sea journey alone, the landing, and then the gathering of the harvest. All these great seabird colonies nest on steep rocky slopes. To catch the young birds before they could fly and escape from a predator, men had to scramble over rocks slippery with sea spray, mossy growth and squelchy build-up of bird droppings.

But such an exercise had to be done to ensure the continuation of a community such as St Kilda on the edge of the world and the edge of starvation. Not all survived to tell the tale. Even Bruinhilda died in her cell, now marked with a cairn nearby. Her body was supposedly discovered with a cormorant's nest in her breast.

Over the centuries the hunt for sea birds during their breeding time must have been a regular occurrence, and the earliest recording of this taking place on Sula Sgeir is from Sir Donald Munro, Dean of the Isles, who when writing in 1549 suggested that it had been an event for at least two hundred years.

Thousands of birds were killed for their flesh, and in the 1869 Preservation of Seabirds Act forbidding any slaughter, a special clause was inserted to exempt St Kildans, as it was accepted that this was an essential way of life.

The method of catching birds may have varied in a small way over the years, as small doses of civilisation filtered through to the islanders, dragging modern ideas in its wake. But basically the chosen men left for the hunting grounds by sea, taking with them all their bedding, water, food and ropes, lived as best they could within the old stone cells which they would frequently have to firstly repair, and caught birds during the day, plucking, singeing and preserving them in salt until enough had been collected and they would transport their booty home.

That the booty is prized so much, and that this harvesting is a rite of passage, a ritual carried out by ancestors as far back as time, can be the only reason for such a tradition to be carried on to this day. St Kilda is deserted, and no men set out from the island today, but one day every year in the summer, ten men take all their needs for a couple of weeks hunting on the island of Sula Sgeir. They come from Lewis, men whose fathers, grandfathers and great-grandfathers have carried out such a hunt. They do not need the food, strictly speaking. The men have other jobs, and support themselves and families in the same way as do men all over the western world. Their aim is to hunt the 'gugas' or gannets, or *Sula Bassana*.

With them they take peats to keep warm, salt to preserve the flesh, food and all their water, as well as a radio to keep them in contact, and finally, a Bible to read each day. Apart from the war years this century, men from Ness have undertaken this ritual every year.

They hitch a lift from a fishing trawler instead of rowing them-selves the 40 miles there, but once on the island, they repair the cells, covering them with plastic, light fires of peat, and then, taking their long catching poles and ropes, proceed to kill around 2,000 'gugas' or young gannets. As the clause was inserted into the 1869 Bill for the protection of seabirds, so, the 1954 Bill exempts the men from Lewis. They are permitted to harvest their birds to this day.

They follow the pattern of untold generations. They scramble over the rocks, often in sheets of unrelenting rain, using their long scissor-like poles to catch a guga round the neck. They choose only birds with a small tuft of feathers on top – those that are old enough to have gained some weight, but not too old to fly. Having snapped the pole round the neck of the victim, the bird is instantly killed, decapitated, handed down the line, and placed in a growing pile. The following morning they are plucked, gutted, slit and singed. The gizzards are placed so that the fat drips onto the peats, creating a blazing fire. The same flat areas are used as have always been used, as too are the same pickling areas.

When the birds have been prepared, they are dipped and rubbed in salt, and placed in a circle on a flat area of ground. The zone is prepared with flat stones, and, as this stage of pickling is vital to the entire harvest, great care is taken to lay out the birds in a great cartwheel, with the feet inwards, and the main part of the breast, carefully covered with skin and salt, forming an overlapping skin round the edge of the circle. Up and up the gugas rise, like an offering to the gods, in the shape of a broch or cairn of birds.

When the harvest is complete, and the fishing boat returns by prior arrangement, all the cells are stripped of possessions, leaving today's helpful addition to such a primitive hunting – polythene coverings – carefully folded up inside. Each man every year adds a stone to his cairn stack, and these symbols of brief human occupation pepper the landscape.

On the quay at the Port of Ness, the most northerly harbour on Lewis, a great gathering crowd greets the returning guga hunters. The men who have hunted the gugas take their quota, other islanders have ordered in advance and form a patient queue to buy a pair of birds. Only then is the surplus sold. A day later, not a trace remains. The harbour is stripped of birds, the equipment has vanished, the men dispersed back to their families and normal jobs, and the gugas are safely stored away salted or in deep freezers around the island. Some keep them for a special occasion, others with larger quantities eat them every month or so during the year.

They are a delicacy, a tribal right, a link with the past, the essence of island lore, adventure, challenge and spirit. They are not necessary for food and survival. To some, in the querying 20th century, it is a slaughter. To the islanders of Lewis, it is a tangible, succulent link with a primitive past. It is not a secretive journey, but a private pilgrimage between island men and their heritage. It whispers like a tale from the history books, but for some reason, inexplicable and perhaps risible to those insensitive to the raw life embodied in the Lewis islanders, it is vital that this hunting of the gugas continues.

THE GREAT SNAKE OF STRONSAY

At the end of September, 1808, with the weather almost calm and quite clear, the occupants of a fishing boat from Stronsay spotted an excited mob of gulls swooping and diving on an object which appeared to be lying on some rocks.

Taking it to be a dead whale, they rowed up to the scene. Although only the centre part was above water, they could see what looked like a mane along its back, and stranger still, six short legs underneath. The owner of the boat, John Peace, managed to lift up one of the legs, but found the body held firmly in the grip of the rocks.

The local landlord heard of this, and immediately contacted his bother, Malcolm Laing, MP JP, a historian and member of the Scottish Bar. Learning that four men had examined the carcass soon after it was stranded, he arranged for them to come over to Kirkwall Magistrates Court and with the assistance of a colleague, he questioned them and took affidavits from each of them.

One of the four, a carpenter by the name of Thomas Fotheringham, had measured the body with his footrule and found it to be almost 55 feet long. One of the 'wings' which he said resembled a goosewing without feathers, was $4^1/2$ feet long. The owner of the boat described the greyish coloured skin as being rough to the touch, but as smooth as velvet if stroked the other way.

After their testimony, the men were shown a drawing of the creature based on their descriptions and which they all agreed was quite accurate (and resembles many artists' impressions of the Loch Ness Monster).

One of the men had collected quantities of bones and bristles from the rapidly decomposing corpse, many of which eventually found their way to the Royal Scottish Museum at Edinburgh.

The scientific fraternity then started to pick over the evidence and a roaring controversy then ensued, with opinions from high learned places coming out in favour of the evidence pointing to nothing more than the remains of a basking shark, and the evidence of the crofters and fishermen being dismissed as ill-educated twaddle. Locals on the islands have clung on to their relics and handed them down the generations, and if nothing else, the bizarre find, and subsequent drawings made on the basis of the original fishermen's descriptions, set a precedent for the new well established image of 'Nessie', with its long neck and huge, lizard-like body.

Well over a hundred years later, at the beginning of the second World War, yet another monster was cast up from the deep midway between Peterhead and Aberdeen.

At first the intrepid fishermen of the 40 foot netter, Seiner, were confident that the weight of the nets indicated a substantial catch... until the nets broke the surface. In place of dozens of silvery fish, only one huge greying mass met their eyes.

The skipper Alexander Strachan, 'Sankey' to all and sundry, was as mystified as his crew, but old fishing superstition was no match for education. Sankey mustered all the modern technology at his disposal, and instructed one of the crew:

'Awa an gie Buchan Ness a shout on the radio. Ask them if onybody't lost an elephant'.

It made a dull end to the story, but he was right. In 1941, a circus elephant had been lost overboard on a trip from Aberdeen to Europe, and ended up in the nets of the Seiner.

BUOYS

Fishermen were ever resourceful. On the Moray coast it was customary to inflate ox bladders, four at a time for use as buoys. These would be tarred and have the owner's initials painted on for identification. Other buoys were made from the blown up skin of a sheep, but the least appealing to twentieth century sensibilities was the use of dog skins. One source declares that the fishermen of Buckie bred dogs specially for this purpose.

SILENT MICE

Creeping along church pews and round pulpits, up choir stalls and along plaques, climbing altar rails and even poised on a Bishop's chair, Scots mice of a very special kind can be seen from Troon to Dornoch and the outer isles.

They are almost all to be glimpsed within ecclesiastical buildings, and are the work of Robert Thompson, born in Kilburn, a north Yorkshire village, in 1876, the son of the local joiner and wheelwright. After five harsh and unpleasant years being apprenticed to a firm of engineers, Robert returned to join his father in the carpenter's workshop, amid the woodworking which he preferred.

It was on a visit to Ripon Cathedral, however, that his vocation shifted somewhat. He glimpsed the work of a late 15th century carver, William Bromflet in the Cathedral, and determined to work in oak, studying the working practices of previous carvers, and rediscovering the adze, an ancient tool which imparted its own special rippling finish to a surface.

Scots writer James Thompson researched the work of this remarkable and prolific carver from his humble origins to the creator of magnificent church furniture, which commenced with a commission from the monks of Ampleforth College. From there he was asked to undertake work for York Minster, carving the prie-dieus, as well as the free standing altar sticks in Westminster Abbey. Both have discreet mice clinging to their base.

In Scotland though, his work carries its mice on traditional hand carving from Troon to Fort Augustus, Pluscarden Abbey, where a mouse can be seen creeping over the edge of a choir stall arm.

Transcending various denominations his work can be searched out at Troon, Moffat, Dornoch, Skye and on the Island of Ensay in the Episcopal Chapel there. In Aberdeen, Robert Thompson created work for the library of Kings College, and further up the coast, at the church of St Peter, or as it is known locally, the Muckle Kirk of Peterhead.

By his death in 1955, Robert Thompson's footsteps were being faithfully followed by his two grandsons, who he had himself trained. To one of these grandsons he explained why his 'signature' of a mouse came about.

'I was carving a beam on a church roof when another carver, Charlie Barker, murmured something about being as poor as church mice, and on the spur of the moment I carved one. Afterwards I decided to adopt the mouse as a trademark, because I thought how a mouse manages to scrape and chew away the hardest wood with its chisel-like teeth and works quietly, with nobody taking much notice. I thought that his was maybe like the workshop hidden away in Hambleton Hills. It is what you might call industry in quiet places, so I included a mouse on all my work.'

His mice sit motionless and poised amid churches all over Scotland.

See under Trysts.

THE SUMMER SHIELINGS

Before the cattle could be driven to the lush pastures of the upper hills for summer grazing, a ceremony would take place. Although this event described by Mrs Barbara Kennedy of Arbroath took place in Perthshire, similar occurrences were enacted all over the Highlands.

This was the taking out for summer of the Cailleach (old

woman) and her family who live high up in the mountains at the head of Glen Lyon in their house of Tigh Nam Bodach.

'This house was a rounded beehive-shaped shelter made of stones and thatched over. Before the cattle were driven to the grazings, fresh thatch would be placed on the roof and any repairs needed to the 'house' would be done. This having been seen to, it was believed no harm would then befall the activities of the shielings. When the herds were moved down in October, the 'family' was carefully returned inside and their 'house' sealed up for winter.'

The Cailleach – she is about 18 inches high – and her family are a group of heavy water-worn stones, shaped like dumbbells. Unpleasant things are supposed to happen if she and her family are disturbed from their winter's nest. Her family is meant to grow at the rate of one every hundred years. Today they number five.

One of the estate workers, for example a shepherd, stalker or keeper, looked after her and her family and home, taking them out in the spring, then securing them away for the winter. This ceremony still takes place.

This is reputed to be a pagan shrine, going back to the Mother Goddess Cult, and could well be the only one surviving in Britain.

ROMANTIC CATTLE TRYSTS

Black cattle, most unlikely purveyors of romance, were instrumental in bringing a legacy of music to Falkirk, which then fanned out across the country.

Even devotees of modern day Falkirk would be hard pressed to admit to its romantic air, but for over fifty years at the end of the 18th century, this was the great trysting gathering place of Scotland. It was the natural funnel through which thousands of cattle, herded down on the old drove roads of Scotland, assembled before the final, but profitable journey to the markets of the south.

From the mundane business of cattle rearing and the harshness and isolation of early Highland farming emerged these high days of music, bards, meetings, parties and general merriment, mingled with a heady collection of bankers, commercial entrepreneurs, and the rough Highlandmen whose only contact with such folk was this yearly event.

From these trysts emerged a fund of romantic music and song, to be passed down from generation to generation.

Although the old Falkirk Tryst was essentially a livestock market, with up to 150,000 animals changing hands, plenty of fiddlers and singers were there too, to provide welcome light relief after the serious business of the day. And of course this being canny, sensible Scotland the local bankers were there in force too.

Why did Falkirk become the centre for this vast market? It was the natural junction of roads leading North and South. In its prime, 30,000 cattle changed hands in a week – 'Scotch runts' to the English, who nevertheless bought them up to be herded south to Smithfield for slaughter. However, Falkirk came to this fame only after the Union of the Crowns in 1707 opened up trade with the English. Before this date, Crieff was the major trysting centre.

Crieff was also a natural venue. Its geographical position, just on the border of the Highland line, made it a mutually agreeable meeting place for Highland drovers and southern buyers, who did not care to venture further north into 'mountain fastnesses'. In addition there was plenty of grazing for the black cattle, the main-stay of the markets for a hundred years.

The main reason for the superiority of these small, hardy cattle known as Scottish blacks, lay chiefly in the high rainfall, especially in the Western Isles, which encouraged pastures more lush than in most parts of Scotland. In addition, the cattle could graze higher up the hills, preserving the precious hay of the foothills for extra fodder. In 1772, about 1,700 head of cattle were exported solely from Islay. The growth of artificial feeds, such as turnips was as yet unknown, and thus the sale of cattle was the essential provider of money with which to buy meal.

Most cattle were killed in the autumn at Michaelmas, just a few being retained to form the basis of next year's breeding stock. This was because it was impossible to feed all the stock over the winter. The surviving few were generally so weak by spring, that they had to be carried out into the fields, an episode which was known evocatively as the 'lifting'.

See the Cailleach at Glen Lyon.

Survival, and therefore hardiness was a more obvious attribute than weight or milk yield.

By the trysting time of August or October, the cattle were at their peak and ready to be led south to be sold.

Alexander McKay, a Scotsman supposedly a spy for the Hanovarian government, passed through Crieff in 1722 and had 'the curiosity to go and see the 30,000 cattle... 30,000 guineas in money to the Highlanders.' One wonders what the distant employers thought about his reconnoitring reports of the proceedings:

'Their attendance (the Highlanders) was very numerous, all in belted plaids, girt like a woman's petticoats down to the knee then thighs and half the leg all bare... all spake Irish; an unintelligible language to the English. However, these poor creatures hired themselves out for a shilling a day to drive the cattle to England, and return home at their own charge.'

Later he added tersely that 'there was not leaving anything loose here, it would have been stolen.'

The policing of the event was carried out by the Drummond family, later Baron Baillie of the estate, and the Duke of Perth always attended the trysts personally and conducted the business of 'watching' with great pomp. The Duke held court and settled disputes, and generally kept order. He rode through the market areas, proclaiming his titles at the boundaries of the property, accompanied by his halbertmen, the 18th century equivalent of henchmen. By the tenor of their charters, a number of feuers (a type of tenant) had to supply strong, stalwart youths armed with Lochaber axes as the law and order force. Long after the tryst had moved to Falkirk and Crieff was a more modest affair, the customs of the halbertmen were still observed. They were entitled to whisky as part of their services, provided they presented their axes as proof of their identity. On one occasion at least, the axe was passed on rapidly down the line to all and sundry, until the whisky server, puzzled by the unusually large numbers, strode down the line and, rather late in the day, discovered the truth.

The halbertmen were a necessary force. The disorderly conduct of the Highlanders was recounted by Mr Laurie, a schoolmaster at the nearby hamlet of Monzie, who remembered them as 'bare-footed, bareheaded, though many of them being old men. Being numerous, they used to enter the houses of the country people, take unceremonious possession of their firesides and beds and carry off their potatoes from fields and gardens, and sometimes even the blankets which afforded them temporary covering for the night.'

Light relief came in the form of music makers and bards, although one Robert Dunn from Sutherland was noted for singing happily of his 'Annie, yellow haired daughter of Donald,' who did not bear the separation with equal patience, and Robert returned to find her wed to his rival, the local carpenter.

The skill, and therefore the profit lay in the ability of the drovers to arrive at Crieff with cattle as plump and fit as when they left home. The cattle were led, not driven the road south, and time was of small importance as the grazing was free on the way.

With the Union of the Crowns in 1707, many changes gradually took place.

Firstly, the opening up of the market to English traders. Secondly, improvements in farming led to the enclosures of pastures, thereby restricting the free grazing. So a more southerly meeting place became more practical, especially for the drovers from Galloway – a productive area – and Falkirk as the obvious junction place for north and south. The Highland drovers, with tolls now being levied on the improved roads, and loss of free grazing, were forced to take a speedier and more direct route south.

Crieff's prominence as a trysting centre was gradually eroded. The Statistical Account of the 1790s noted wryly that the decline was partly due 'to the removal of the noble family's interest in the market, and restraints of cattle passing occurred which justice and patriotism would have induced to prevent... had they been residing here.' But in the end it was conceded that Crieff had lost; 'too true it is; that for several years this Mercet hath been dwindling away.' Falkirk was the new centre.

In addition Crieff suffered further losses. Passing drovers left before noon to avoid paying dues, one shilling a score or one penny the head, and the mere 1,000 beasts which now reached Crieff were bought by local Scots butchers or graziers.

Trade at Falkirk for the last ten years of the 18th century was brisk. During the height of the Napoleonic Wars, prices soared to £18 and then £28 per head in the effort to feed the growing army and navy. But the massive rearing of cattle in the north was already on the wane. Wool was in bigger demand, and sheep were replacing cattle in the Highlands. Their progress was slow but sure from about 1759 onwards until the collapse of the cattle market in 1815. With it came the end of the bards, halbertmen, music making and great commercial gatherings of Highlandmen. The end of the great trysting days.

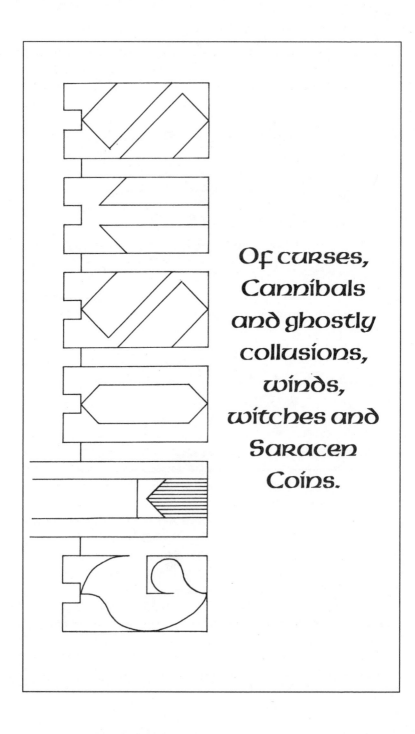

Of curses,
Cannibals
and ghostly
collusions,
winds,
witches and
Saracen
Coins.

Tales of curse blighting Scottish families are legion, and exist long after religious influence should have smothered such beliefs. But superstition and pagan beliefs were never far separated from religion. There is one common thread which runs through almost all of the known incidents of curses, spells and witchcraft. The vast majority all resulted from the 'eye' or words of women.

FARQUHARSON OF INVERCAULD

The House of Invercauld is a splendid edifice on Deeside, neighbours to the Queen at Balmoral, but it was at Braemar Castle, close to Braemar on the A93, that much of the stormy history of the Farquharson family is rooted. It was from this castle, described as the Castleton of Mar, that the Farquharsons entertained Queen Victoria to the annual Gathering, and generations before, that they had left to fight and spread their might over their harassed neighbours.

That the family still occupy the estate to this day is the most remarkable fact about Invercauld, considering the curse which was inflicted upon it.

The origins of this curse appear to be rooted in fact, if not accurately in time.

In the skirmishes between the occupiers of the lands of the north east in the 15th or perhaps 16th centuries – or just perhaps later than this – a Lamont of Inverey was hanged on a pine tree. The pine tree stood on a knoll just to the west of Mar Lodge Bridge.

The bare bones of the story go thus.

Lamont of Inverey, a hamlet which lies west of Braemar, had assisted the McIntosh's in one of their battles, and when the said McIntosh's were beating a retreat, left Lamont to the mercy of his close neighbours, against whom he had previously been at odds. Now left alone, he was a vulnerable man.

It is surprising that the powerful Farquharsons and their accomplices needed any further proof of guilt before they hung Lamont, but perhaps they decided on a belt and braces approach to justice. The tale describes how the Farquharsons 'planted' some sheep in one of Lamont's lime kilns, which were then 'found' and therefore rendered Lamont guilty of sheep stealing. This was a very convenient crime, as hanging was the traditional remedy.

Lamont must of course have been unwilling to be dragged off to the stout pine tree for his hanging, but his widowed mother was devastated, and pleaded with the Farquharsons to save her son's life, promising they could take anything they wished in return for sparing him. But it was all to no avail, and when the hangman's rope was tightened she cursed the Farquharsons, or Clan Fhionnlaidh's whom she considered prime movers in the deed.

> 'This tree will flourish high and broad,
> Green as it grows today,
> When from the banks o' the bonnie Dee,
> Clan Fhionnlaidh's all away'.

At the time, the Farquharsons owned huge areas of the Dee valley, and appeared invincible, and their fighting spirit carried them along for some time. But it was not to last.

You can judge for yourself if you look in the Invercauld Aisle in the Braemar Churchyard at all but one small section of the family.

> 'Sacred to the memory of John Farquharson of Invercauld, who died in 1750. Sacred also to the memory of James Farquharson of Invercauld his son who died 24th June 1805; and Amelia, Lady Sinclair, his spouse (daughter of Lord James Murray) who died in 1779. They had eleven children, all of whom with the exception of the youngest, Catherine, died before them. Mary, Matilda, Jane, John and George lie interred with their parents in the ground joining; Charlotte in Arnhall; Fanny at Lisbon; and Amelia, Margaret and Ann in the burying ground in North Leith.'

To this day, the inheritor of the Farquharsons of Invercauld has rarely passed by direct descent.

GIPSIES CURSE

Quoted from the *Newcastle Weekly Chronicle*, 1898.

A Gipsy's Revenge.

At Jedburgh in the year 1718 a gipsy youth, one of the Yetholm band, was tried for some transgression against the Border laws. The chief bailie of magistrates on that bench that day happened to be Sir William Kerr of Greenhead, who ordered the lad to be detained in custody for a short period. A few days afterwards the boy's mother, in revenge for what she considered an injury, set fire to the house of Bridgend, the ancient seat of the Greenhead family, which was burned to the ground.

The mother was soon captured and taken before Sir William, who ordered her to be nailed through the ears to a post in Jedburgh, at the same time expressing his regret that it did not lie in his power to rid the country of the tribe of vagabonds. How long the woman remained at the post is not known, but long enough to utter the curses against the inflictor that his heirs might die childless and his wife become a widow. That is just what happened.

Sir William died in 1721 and was succeeded by his only son who died shortly after the year 1726 without issue, when the baronetcy became extinct.

Possibly foreseeing this, Sir William, granted to his cousin Andrew Kerr, who attained his 100th birthday in 1721 that portion of the Primside estate known as Hoselaw. The Patriarch of the clan, however, only enjoyed his inheritance for three short years, dying at his seat Blegdie, near Edinburgh, on December 2 1724 aged 102 years leaving no issue. His remains were interred in the picturesque church-yard at Pencaitland, where an elaborate monument in the form of a sarcophagus bearing his arms was erected to his memory, and remains to this day in a good state of preservation.

The 'vagrants' about which Sir William was so derisive were travellers who based themselves in Yetholm (see chapter on Royalty) but they clearly lived up to their wandering name, as an account in the *Northern Scot* of 30 September 1893 testifies.

Dr Gordon of Braebirnie, Elgin wrote to the paper telling of his visit with a friend to a cave along the coast.

'near the fishing village of Hopeman, is known locally as Hell's Hole. It has been for time immemorial the temporary shelter of otherwise houseless wanderers and particularly of gipsies and tinkers. Early in the century, when the late William Young resided on his property, Inverugie in the neighbourhood of this notable cave, a friend from the Borders was on a visit to him. One day they went to this gipsy abode and had no sooner entered than one of the inmates came up and cordially addressed the border gentleman, who received the salutation with such equal heartiness as naturally made Mr Young draw up, so as to indicate his desire to know who his friend was. The explanation was at once given that he was a respectable merchant and in good society in Yetholm; but that in his early years he had been accustomed to this nomadic life; and that now, like the migratory bird, he could not resist the desire of occasionally revisiting the caves and renewing the customs of days of other years,'

SAUNIE BANE

The name has been passed down true enough. Alexander Bean was the son of a respectable ditcher and hedger in the County of Haddington, now East Lothian. As to the date of this story, it is lost in the mythology of generations of whispered story telling around the fires of centuries.

From Haddington Alexander Bean then travelled on to Galloway, to which he went with a woman of ill repute and together they settled in a remote part of the Galloway shore.

There they occupied a cave and lived a simple life, by robbing and then eating some unfortunate folk passing by. They had a large family and in due course, as they grew up, brother married sister and begat more Beans, or Banes, as another version of the story names them. Their cannibalistic tendency increased as the numbers grew.

The effect of this cannibalistic colony had long been felt in the surrounding country, but the culprits were unknown. So many wayfarers had disappeared that suspicion fell on some inn keepers and, for good measure, several were hung, but still the disappearances continued.

Finally, one evening as dusk was falling, a farmer was returning on his pony from Laurencekirk Fair, his wife on the pillion behind him, when suddenly, a crowd of Banes rose up out of the moorland around them. The farmer defended himself desperately, but despite his efforts, his wife was torn from the pillion.

In an instant her throat was cut – the Banes, men and women were drinking her blood with 'as great a gust as it had been wine' (according to a vivid mid-Victorian description) and she was ripped open and her entrails were torn out. At this, the farmer made a final desperate lunge and broke away, just as a large party of country folk came into view. They were also returning from the fair. Presumably seeing so many folk arriving, the Banes scattered, abandoning the woman's corpse.

On hearing the farmer's account, the whole party made for Glasgow, where they notified the Magistrates, who sped off to inform King James I.

King James himself, with a large body of men, arrived to search the coast, but to no avail. The Banes seemed to have vanished.

The search party had passed an apparently shallow cave mouth and were far down the shore, thinking of abandoning their search, when they heard the bloodhounds they had brought with them baying and whining at the mouth of the cave. Tentatively wending their way through the narrow entrance of the cave, they found it widening, and a mile and a half inside found the Banes, amid a scene akin to a medieval vision of hell. Human limbs steeped in tubs, or were hanging smoked on hooks – and tubs and boxes full of watches, rings, pistols, snuff boxes and jewellery.

Fifty-eight members of the Banes were captured amidst this

grisly scene. The human remains were decently buried in the sand at the mouth of the cave and the party returned to Edinburgh, tossing the Banes into the Tolbooth, before executing them the next day without trial.

The old Scots tale describes the executions in sparse, understated terms:

'the men did their hauns and legs cut off and left tae bleed taa daith: the weemen and bairns, hiving watched this, were burnt in three saiveral fires, a' cursin' tae their laust gasp'.

THE KISHORN DWARFS

The early 20th century Finlayson gravestone in the old churchyard at Lochcarron still stands, carved by brothers Finlay and John for themselves, from stone they had previously quarried for just this purpose.

The stone came from the romantically named Baelach na Ba, or Hill of the Cattle, beyond which is the peninsula of Applecross. The brothers and their only sister, Mary, were born and brought up at the foot of the pass, in a house called Bruach a Ghoirtean near Tornapress, which sits at the junction of the famous mountain road with that of Kishorn to Shieldaig.

Later on when in middle age, the trio took up residence on Ardarroch shore where their cottage still stands.

The distance between these two houses can be no more than a few miles, and although it would not have been unusual for folk such as them to stay close to home all their lives, the Finlayson trio were much travelled, and had met no less a personage than Queen Victoria. Born around the 1820s the three Finlaysons all lived to a ripe old age, and it is said that when around 1915 the last to die, Finlay, the schoolmaster line the children up by the roadside to pay their last respects to the 'gille beag' as he left his house which was known locally as 'tigh nan gillean beags' or, the dwarfs house.

All three siblings were dwarfs.

Local legend whispers that they were born dwarfs because of a curse dealt out to the parents by the jilted girlfriend of their father.

The marriage is reputed to have taken place at Cnoc-nan-Uainon, amid the Applecross hills.

Stan Forrester, a local writer, says that 'we can perhaps surmise that there was some irregularity about the marriage, or some objection to it. We can perhaps conjecture that he results of the marriage were some visitation on the couple for their self-willed determination to go ahead with it.'

Certainly there seems to be evidence that when the third child was born as a dwarf, the poor mother 'went off her heid', and there were no more babies.

The story then skips on until March 1846, when reports start appearing in the *Inverness Journal* and *Inverness Courier* about 'The Highland Dwarfs'.

'These diminutive creatures, three in number, two lads and a girl, all of one family in Ross shire, are at present at Ardnagask near Beauly. Mr W. Mackenzie, the tacksman of Ardnagask has engaged them for twelve months and is shortly to take them to London for exhibition. Hitherto the dwarfs earned a livelihood by going about in their native country purchasing eggs for parties engaged in exploiting them. Their father was a shepherd, and his death took place twelve years ago. He was of small stature, but their mother, who is still alive and rents a small croft in Lochcarron is about the middle size.'

The report goes on to refer to them as MacFindlay – which was no doubt a more Scottish sounding name than Finlayson, and that the brothers were then aged 22 and 20, Mary being 18. They were double-jointed, and Mr Mackenzie had apparently engaged a piper, and taught them to dance, sing and chant Gaelic melodies, all in preparation for their trip to London.

'He has indeed spared no expense in teaching and fitting out these small specimens of humanity and we have little doubt that they will be regarded by the Sassenachs as rare objects of curiosity.'

Somewhat unctuously, the paper adds that

'it is scarcely necessary to add that Mr Mackenzie is a highly respectable, intelligent individual, and that the best wishes of his friends in the North accompany him on his new undertaking.'

The tours lasted but a few years, after which the three lived together in tranquillity for many years, clearly never hankering after their brief years of fame.

MISS FREER AND THE BALLECHIN INVESTIGATION

In the National Library of Scotland there is a copy of the first edition of *The Alleged Haunting of B——— House*, first published in 1899, which came from the library of Lord Rosebery, to whom it had been presented by Lord Bute.

The mysterious house, Ballechin, was situated on the Tay close to Dunkeld in Perthshire. It was a classic Georgian house and the property of an old Highland family called Steuart.

The hauntings first came to light during the ownership of Major Robert Steuart (1806–76) who had retired from the East India Company in 1850. He never married and was regarded as an eccentric because of his excessive fondness of dogs, of which he kept a large number, and his belief in spiritual return. It was locally said that he himself had declared that he would return to haunt Ballechin after his death, probably in the form of a black spaniel, of which he was particularly fond, and this could have been the reason that all his fourteen dogs were shot after his death. Malicious local talk also linked his name with that of his young housekeeper, Miss Sarah Nicolson, who died at Ballechin on the 14 July 1873 at the age of 27, and was buried there. Major Steuart arranged that his body was to be buried adjacent to hers upon his own death.

In August 1892 Lord Bute heard about the odd bumps in the night at Ballechin when a priest Father Patrick Hayden was visiting Falkland Palace in Fife, of which Lord Bute was the hereditary keeper. Father Hayden had been staying at Ballechin during the previous month of July and heard strange noises and had seen, between waking and sleeping, a momentary vision of a brown crucifix. A year later Father Hayden met a Miss Yates, who twelve years previously had been a governess at Ballechin and left because 'so many people complained of queer noises in the house.' Father Hayden reported this to Lord Bute, who in turn told the story to one Ada Goodrich Freer, an American who made much of her investigations into the misty world of psychic happenings in Scotland.

Accordingly, Lord Bute was coerced by Miss Freer and some of her associates into spending a week at the house to note down what happened.

Her record became the book, *The Alleged Hauntings of B——House* and eventually the blueprint for a well known book written by Harry Price *The Most Haunted House in England.*

Miss Freer and her associates strongly believed in the haunting of the house, and produced all sorts of evidence to prove that doors had holes knocked into them mysteriously overnight and many types of strange noises were heard. But the scandal caused by the book, which alluded to Major Steuart's relationship with his housekeeper, the collusion of Lord Bute, and the eccentricity of Miss Freer, who stuck to her story for the rest of her life only served to ridicule the entire story.

Many other tenants of the house heard strange happenings and testified to the peculiar atmosphere. But modern day visitors will be disappointed. The house was demolished in 1963.

THE WITCHCRAFT TRIAL OF MRS DUNCAN

What made a typical witch? A lithe, young lassie? An old crone living in a hovel? Mrs Helen Duncan fitted neither of these images at her trial in the Old Bailey in London. She was accused under the Witchcraft Act of 1735, where the maximum punishment was just a year's imprisonment.

A description of Mrs Duncan at the trial conjured up a vision of a largish lady – twenty stone or so in weight – who had a 'large, bovine, reddish face', a housewife, and was married with six children. She had drifted into the business of witchcraft when into her thirties. Originally having hailed from Perthshire, she had lived most of her married life in Edinburgh. She claimed to be able to emulate, when in a trance and under the control of 'guides', those from the dead. These would materialise in the actual physical form of a spirit, not indeed the flesh and blood, but in a strange semi-physical, semi-spiritual substance known as 'ectoplasm', which exudes from their body.

Such was her fame and popularity amid her devotees, or those who were already drifting towards such a trend, that she travelled around conducting meetings where she would 'meet' the dead on behalf of her clients. From these meetings she would gain financially, having sold seats to attend her 'visitings'. Her meetings took place in the houses of sympathisers, and were carefully broadcast by whispered word of mouth.

But the downfall of Mrs Duncan came about in the unlikely setting of Portsmouth, through a young Royal Naval Lieutenant Worth, who attended one of her meetings. In a nutshell, young Mr Fowler felt he had been deceived. He didn't believe for a moment that she was telling the truth, and worse, he had been cheated out of a hard earned 12s and 6d. For this all took place in 1944.

That a witch should be put on trial at the Old Bailey in the midst of the 20th century was indeed distraction for a war weary public, who crowded round the blitz damaged building to pick up all the nuances of the trial.

Indeed, it was mainly the two world wars in which so many had suffered bereavement, which led to the rise of pundits like Mrs Duncan. The upsurge in spiritualism, which is nearer to the doctrine practised by Mrs Duncan and her like, was directly as a result of the innumerable mourners who sought out possible contact with their deceased loved ones. All might have been well if Mrs Duncan had not sought to make a pretty penny from the desperation and misery of her clients. But she had not reckoned on coming across someone as strong willed as Lieutenant Worth. He felt aggrieved that such a trickster was gaining from something which was clearly sham, and told the police.

Mrs Duncan must never even in her considerable imaginative powers conjured up the sequence of coincidences which led her from an upstairs room in Portsmouth to the dock at the Old Bailey and national fame.

It is a pity that nothing is known of Mrs Duncan's early life, and how she was caught up in the world of spiritualism. But by 1931 she was investigated by a Spiritualist Society in London, who damned her claims and declared her abilities as a materialising medium quite false. This had the result of making her a martyr, and she was immediately surrounded by defenders who lifted her status remarkably.

Then in 1933 she was hitting the headlines in Edinburgh for obtaining money by false pretences – about which, it could be said, her supernatural abilities, should perhaps have warned her. The main thrust of the accusations was that a spirit called Peggy, materialised by Mrs Duncan, was built not of ectoplasm, but of a piece of thin white cloth, which was actually gripped and torn by one of the audience. Again, as in 1931, her admirers gathered round, perhaps even helped pay the fine, and the fame of Mrs Duncan simply received yet another boost from her conviction.

By the time she met her downfall in 1944, she was demanding and receiving as much as £104 for a week's engagement.

The scene of her engagement in Portsmouth was the 'Master Temple Psychic Centre'. This was the upstairs room of a Mr and Mrs Homer, a very ordinary, middle-aged couple, who owned and ran the chemist's shop on the ground floor at street level.

Into this shop one day in December 1943 walked Lieutenant Worth, the young naval officer who was curious about Spiritualism. Mrs Homer enthused about Mrs Duncan, who was engaged to appear in the upstairs room the following week. Among the marvels which Mrs Homer described was that the ectoplasm Mrs Duncan produced was so vital that, when it rushed back into her body after being built up as a spirit form, it swept with it all sorts of objects from the form into Mrs Duncan's body, like a vacuum cleaner.

Convinced that this was well worth seeing, he paid his 12s and 6d and bought a ticket. Then telling Mrs Homer about his friend Surgeon Lieutenant Fowler, who was very sceptical about spiritualism, he was exhorted to;

'Bring him along to see Mrs Duncan. I'll give him a seat in the front row and scare him stiff.' So another 12s and 6d changed hands.

On 14 January the two men duly climbed the stairs to what was imminently to become the most famous upstairs room in Portsmouth, and sat down to enjoy the proceedings.

The chairs formed a semicircle, and were marked with the names of the intended sitters. Inadvertently, the young officers changed places.

They faced a corner of the room which was cordoned off with a dark curtain. Mrs Homer then passed round a black frock, a pair of black knickers and a pair of black shoes – all the 'seance' clothes of Mrs Duncan. The sitters agreed that these items had nothing concealed inside them, and then two women from the audience were invited to go and watch Mrs Duncan undress and put on her seance clothes, even searching her hair to make sure that there was nothing concealed.

The seance then progressed in what was a normal manner, with a sing-song, the Lords Prayer, and only a dim red light, made even less so because it was additionally draped with a scarlet scarf. But things started to go wrong when Mrs Duncan, having been primed by Mrs Homer about this sceptical young man also being a doctor, proceeded to discuss various medical problems with a client. If Surgeon-Lieutenant Fowler had known the answers, Lieutenant Worth certainly did not, and this triggered off their suspicions. All the homework done by Mrs Homer and related to Mrs Duncan came to nought.

At the realisation that this questioning was less than successful, Mrs Duncan turned her attentions elsewhere in the audience. Mrs Duncan had a seance guide called Albert, and he assisted things along. A cat was produced for one of the sitters, or at least there was a miaow from the cabinet in the corner, and a small white object appeared between the curtains a few feet from the ground. It was followed by a parrot which was recognised by one of the sitters in the audience as Dear Old Bronco, and brought pleasant memories by saying 'Pretty Polly' just as in life. Next Albert produced an ectoplasmic rabbit out of the cabinet, and then humans 'appeared' until Mrs Duncan stumbled out of the cabinet and was taken away to be dressed again.

The entire sequence revolved round this mysterious piece of ectoplasm, which materialised as a spirit. Lieutenant Worth was asked what he thought of the seance, and he replied that every time a spirit or ectoplasm disappeared behind the curtains, there was a rustling sound.

Privately, he was totally disillusioned by the entire performance, annoyed at losing 12s and 6d and determined to inform the police.

Acting with their knowledge and suggestions, he bought another ticket, and at the appropriate moment, shone a torch on the hapless Mrs Duncan, who, instead of reclining behind the curtains in a trance, was seen to be desperately clutching not the surreal ecto-plasm but a length of white cloth. As a policeman lunged up the stairs to assist in the melee, the cloth was snatched out of Worth's hands and smuggled away into the audience. But it was the begin-ning of the end for Mrs Duncan, whose mystic powers had been wafted away on a young naval officer's suspicions.

After much head scratching amongst the law officers, she was charged under the Witchcraft Act.

Later, at the trial, it was not so much that anyone doubted that Mrs Duncan and her followers genuinely believed in her powers, but the money-making motives behind them.

The first witness for the defendant was a Mr Kirkby, retired busi-nessman, who announced that everybody has a spirit guide, a state-ment which caused the Recorder to express regret that he had not one to help him find his way through this evidence. He also told remarkable stories of Mrs Duncan's feats in the past, and rejected with scorn the suggestion of the 1931 investigation that the 'spirits' were made up of butter muslin, swallowed by her before a seance and then regurgitated by her. Other witnesses spoke of seances in which Mary Queen of Scots spoke. From all over the country supporters of Mrs Duncan came to speak on her behalf.

An electrical draughtsman from Blackpool followed with more reminiscences, and after him came Sir James Harris JP, an Edinburgh journalist, who had met the spirit of Conan Doyle.

And so it went on, until the Recorder, having resisted many attempts by the queues of defence witnesses to elaborate on their experiences, then asked the jury if they wished Mrs Duncan to give a demonstration of a seance. They briskly refused and within half an hour of being dismissed to consider the verdict, returned to bring in a verdict of guilty. Mrs Duncan was sentenced to a year in prison.

The only secret never revealed at the trial was quite how this piece of fabric, meant to represent a spirit, but claimed to be ecto-plasm was concealed by Mrs Duncan. The only possibility was that, after undressing, being searched and then sitting in her curtained cubicle under the very dim red light, one of her accomplices managed to smuggle it in and out. But it was not only the secret left at the end of the astonishing trial under the Witchcraft Act, other than the strong feeling that those who believed in her powers had not for one moment, even under the scrutiny of one of the highest courts in the land, been shaken in their beliefs.

The Constable of Portsmouth was called to give details of the defendant's record to date, and reported that not only was her Edinburgh conviction against her, but he said, she had been reported to the police for announcing the loss of a warship 'before the news was made public'. No more was ever said about this accu-sation, but it leaves, amid the mockery of the ectoplasm, the undressing, the spiriting up of parrots and cats, just a frisson of uncertainty.

WHATEVER HAPPENS TO OLD MOONS?

The name of Maviston still appears on maps, although the inhabi-tants of the village which supposedly stood there until the beginning of the last century would certainly not wish to be reminded of the reason for their fame. They laboured under the unflattering label of the Mavistoun Gouks, meaning those of simple, stupid and overtly superstitious mentality. Perhaps the poor Mavistoun Gouks were all of those things, but there is one story attributed to them which does much to endear their thinking to us, and is an outstandingly logical answer.

The question was in connection with the moon, and was thought telling enough to warrant a mention in the *History of Moray and Nairn*, published in 1897.

'It is said that once a fisherman found a horseshoe on the beach. It was the first that he had ever seen, and all the wise men in the little community gathered together to examine it. One of them at last hazarded the opinion that it was a bit of the moon – in fact a new moon. This view was promptly contradicted by the man, who being the oldest, was regarded as the wisest among them.

'A moon it was,' he believed, 'but it could not be a new moon, otherwise it would be up in the sky.'

'For himself, he had often wondered what became of the old moons. This settled it. The old moons fell to the earth and this was one of them.'

THE MUCH TRAVELLED LEE PENNY

When the plague broke out in Newcastle during the latter part of the 17th century, the disease having been transported south from the Borders, the city fathers knew of but one certain saviour.

They were prepared to offer the enormous guarantee of £6,000 in order to borrow the 'Lee Penny' from the Lockharts of Lee House, Lanarkshire. So convinced were the people of Newcastle that the famous penny would protect them from the plague, and as a measure of their desperation to save themselves from its ravages, they also offered to forfeit the deposit in order to keep the charm within their city walls. The Lockharts refused point blank. The charm was returned to them and remains in their possession for another three hundred years to this day.

The Lockharts had acquired this much valued and famous talisman during a romantic, but ill-fated expedition to the Holy Land. Sir Symon Loccard (the earliest spelling of the name) was accompanying Lord James Douglas, who was leading an expedition to bury the heart of Robert the Bruce. In this great age of chivalry, Bruce had hoped that he would be able to make amends with his maker by taking part in a crusade. He wished to absolve the great sin he had committed when battling for the Scottish throne by murdering the Red Comyn in a convent chapel near Dumfries. Unable to fulfil this ambition before he realised that he was about to die, he instructed his loyal knights to remove his heart and take it to the Holy Land.

Accordingly, Lord James placed the precious heart in a silver casket, and with the relic hung around his neck, set out for the Holy Land.

The Knights were side-tracked in their expedition and entered into a fierce engagement with the Moors in Spain. When he saw another knight, Sir William St Clare of Roslin surrounded by enemy forces, Sir Douglas flung the casket towards him crying.

'Be thou in the van brave heart as thou was ever wont, and Douglas will follow or die.'

The battle was won, the casket saved, but Sir Douglas was killed, leaving the mantle of leadership to fall upon Sir Symon Loccard. Disheartened by this first foray, the expedition returned home, and it was at this time that the name of Loccard was changed to Lockheart for a while, in honour of this act of bravery, before finally settling as Lockhart, which it has remained to the present day. The heart of Robert the Bruce, having never finished its journey to the Holy Land is reputed to have been buried under the east wing of the chancel of Melrose Cathedral.

But it was also from this ill-fated expedition that the coin was acquired. It is said to have been given to him as part of the ransom to pay for the release of the Moorish chief whom he had captured. After seizing the wealthy Emir, Sir Symon Loccard was confronted by his desperate mother, for whose release she was prepared to pay generously in precious gold and silver. The story tells how the lady accidentally dropped a jewel, and, suspicious of the speed with which she bent down to snatch this stone, Sir Symon suspected that this small item could well be more valuable than the gold and silver already offered.

Demanding the jewel as part of the ransom, she reluctantly surrendered it to him explaining that the stone was indeed a treasure worth more than all the considerable wealth she had already offered, as it was a remedy to cure bleeding and fever, the bite of a mad dog, and sickness in horses and cattle.

The Lee Penny as it became known is in fact a red stone of triangular shape set in an Edward I shilling coin, clearly an insertion which took place at a much later date, and leapt to fame as Sir Walter

Scott's 'Talisman'. Sir Walter, though, made no secret of his embell-
ishment of the story. Eventually it was attached to a silver chain, and
kept in a circular silver casket.

For centuries it was credited with healing powers; water in which
it had been dipped being regarded as a cure for diseased cattle. For
people, it was held to possess almost magical qualities of curing. The
coin would be drawn three times round a cup of water, then three
times dipped in the water, which the patient then drank, or applied
to a wound or sore. Even after the Reformation, when such talis-
mans were contrary to accepted belief and smacked of witchcraft,
the power of the Lee Penny was still observed.

Tales of its properties travelled far. In 1629 the 'routting evil'
attacked cattle in Scotland, especially around Haddington and a
deputation travelled to beg the use of the Lee Penny to stop this
plague. The Laird of the time, Sir James, would not allow the penny
to travel at all, but offered instead to fill flagons of water in which the
penny had been swirled. The cattle were cured, but in keeping with
the suspicions of the day, one poor woman, Isobel Young of East
Barns, was accused of witchcraft and burnt at the stake.

Even right into the 19th century, it was common practice for a
bottle of Lee water to be kept in byres as a precaution in case the sickness should strike, and in 1824, a Yorkshire man came all the way on
foot to ask for water with which to treat his cattle.

In the early part of the 20th century, the Lee Penny was still
playing its part. Sir Simon Lockhart was entertaining some guests at
a shooting party, when they discovered at lunch time that they were
without a bottle opener, whereupon the guest, attempting to open
the bottle with a knife, let it slip and gashed his wrist.

In the evening, by then feeling faint and still unable to staunch the
blood, he asked Sir Simon to call a doctor. Sir Simon was not to allow
the Lee Penny to rest unused. He rescued the coin from its safe,
swirled it around in the water, bathed his guest's wrist, and by the
morning, but one small dry scar was to be found.

To this day, the precious Lee Penny, packed into its elaborately
embellished silver box, remains in the possession of the Lockhart
family, and resides in a safe.

THE BABY STONE OF BURGHEAD

The wall round the churchyard at Burghead, north of Elgin on the Moray coast, contains a cup-like hollow, four inches wide, two inches deep and quite round and smooth. According to local legend, the hollow has been formed by generations of children striking this spot with a stone from the beach, then quickly putting their ear to the place. The sounds that are supposed to be heard are variously claimed to be those of a baby crying, the crooning of a granny hushing her child to sleep, or a rocking cradle.

It is quite a likely tale. For, all local children believed that beneath this stone was the spot from where themselves and all later babies were meant to have firstly emerged.

THE LADY WHO SOLD WINDS
AND THE TALE OF GRANNY KEMPOCH

Betty Miller lived in Stromness, Orkney at the beginning of the last century and eked out her livelihood by selling winds to mariners. Such was her reputation, and she was held in such awe that those who found themselves in a boat with a sailor who had neglected to make his purchase would turn back for the man to make his amends with Betty and part with his silver.

Sir Walter Scott records that 'she boiled her kettle, gave the barque advantage of her prayers, for she disdained all unlawful arts. The wind, thus petitioned for, was sure to arrive, though sometimes the mariners had to wait some time for it.' The eminent Sir Walter also noted that the clever lady lived on the windswept prow of the steep hill above the town, and 'for exposure might have been the abode of Eolus himself.'

Betty Miller lived to be nearly 100, and although described by a visiting mariner as being withered and dried up like a mummy, was still dispensing advice for financial reward and much revered up until her death.

That the winds could be controlled was a well established belief. Perhaps Betty Miller had heard about Granny Kempoch and adopted her powers.

Granny Kempoch was never a mother or a granny. She is a tall rock of around six feet, standing proud and watching over the Firth of Clyde, clearly marked on maps close to Greenock. Her position, just on the point where ships would have turned out of the Clyde and into the open sea, was clearly significant to sailors of old.

G.L. Gomme, writing in the early 19th century tells us that

'At one time an unknown saint was wont to dispense favourable winds to those who paid for them, and unfavourable to those who did not put confidence in his powers – a tradition which seems to have been carried on by the Innerkip witches who were tried in 1662, and some portions of which still linger among the sailors at Greenock.

'In former times sailors and fishermen sought to ensure good fortune on the sea by walking seven times round the stone. While making their rounds they carried in their hand a basket of sand, and at the same time uttered an eerie chant.'

Telling Tales of Tartan. Of Bondagers, Glovers, Scudders and Skeklers and Eerie Forms of Forgotten Dress, Precious Pearls and Puzzling Patterns.

Is there indeed another country which has given its name to so many widely assorted patterns? Tartan, Paisley and Fair Isle are but three of the most famous. They are instantly recognisable the world over. While in other countries national dress has been relegated to museums, worn only on ceremonial occasions, or trundled out for major events, the Scottish national pattern, tartan, is now more popular than ever and appears in more permutations each year.

But from where did tartan derive? The misty regions of Highland glens? And more curiously, where did those most Scottish of patterns, Paisley and Fair Isle spring from? The answers are surprising.

But if these patterns are well known, albeit in secret and unexpected origins, what of the other, less familiar Scottish oddities, of skeklers dress, tatted socks, bondagers costumes, the glovers dress and the scarlet robes of St Andrews University students? From where did these forms of dress derive, and why did some vanish, and some survive?

TARTAN

If there is one pattern and fabric which is famous the world over, tartan must be almost at the top of the list. It has been fought over, banned, worn in secret, jealously guarded and used as uniforms, furnishings, painted on china, 'adopted' by other nations and re-named 'plaid'.

From where does the word tartan derive? The answers are certainly not clearcut.

Either from a derivation of the French 'tiretaine' or possibly the Gaelic 'tarsuinn' meaning across, which could refer to the weaving process. The Gaelic word for tartan is 'breacan' which means speckled or partly coloured, so one explanation for use of 'tarsuinn' is that the word tartan at its earliest did not refer to the familiar check as we know it, but to a type of cloth, possibly quite plain.

But the first myth which can be destroyed with confidence is the sheer age of tartan. Compared with Celtic and Pictish designs, tartan is a relative newcomer. Although tartan is of an abstract repetitive design, the same as the basis of all Celtic art, there is not a shred of evidence for tartan being worn before 1538. At that date there is a definite account of an order for James V, amongst which is three ells (an ell is an arm's length or about 1¼ yards) of 'Helend tertane, to be hoiss for Kingis Grace.' The most feasible explanation, according to the experts, was that this would be of a simple two colour check, and would have been made into, not a kilt, but a pair of stockings, socks or trews...

Another myth is that the tartans originated in the Highlands, with each clan forming its own tartan and fighting other clans in their own recognisable check, which would have been assigned by their clan chief.

The truth is that tartans most probably found their way from the two colours, brown or black, interspersed with white or cream check, known as the Shepherds Check. This was woven in the Lowlands by the local weavers from local sheep.

Then comes a recording by no less a Frenchman than the historian Beaugue, who describes 'light coverings of wool of many colours' worn by Highlanders at a siege in Flanders, and a woodcut of 1631 depicts Highlanders, possibly mercenary soldiers, who were fighting in the army of Gustavus Adolphus wearing what passes for tartan. One soldier, though, is distinctly seen wearing a recognisable belted plaid, the early forerunner of the kilt.

But then there is a misty gap between tartan appearing as dress and the different clan tartans of the Highlanders.

How did this come about? No one knows for certain. Gradually though, old records show that by the time of Dundee's campaign in 1691, sections of his men wore recognisably the same cloth. Most likely, it was a sensible economy, as the chiefs ordered large quantities.

In 1703, Martin Martin, historian and inveterate traveller wrote a *Description of the Western Isles of Scotland* in which he said that

'Every isle differs from each other in their Fancy of making Plads, as to the Stripes in Breadth, and Colours. This Humour is as different thro the main Land of the Highlands, in-so-far that they who have seen those Places are able, at the first View of a Man's Plad, to guess the Place of his Residence.'

But it was less likely that this was as a result of clan or tribal pride, far more probable that the colours were culled from plants growing in that area, the skill with which the dyer would obtain the colours, and the making of a large quantity of the same cloth, for reasons of economy.

The truth is that no one really knows.

What is far more relevant to the survival of tartan today, and its popularity, is that the wearing of tartan hit upon a major crisis after the uprising of 1745. The wearing of tartan was banned, and as happens so often when there is a crisis, the weaving, wearing, and sheer interest in tartan took a huge upswing. Although forbidden in the Highlands until 1782, it was ironically introduced as a recruiting inducement for the Army.

Then an enterprising weaving firm in Bannockburn, William Wilson and Son, founded in the middle of the 18th century, made the wearing of tartan of all types possible with their wide use of colours and pattern, and then gradually the wearing of one's own tartan became more and more popular. Rather unromantically, Wilson's wrote to numerous Lairds and Lords suggesting various colour combinations, which is how many of our clan tartans came to be chosen.

Then in 1822 the most magnificent modern marketing exercise for tartan burst upon a surprised Edinburgh public. Quite unwittingly, this was carried out by the major players in the drama, Sir Walter Scott and General Stewart of Garth (near Glenlyon) who became the supporting cast for the principal player, King George IV. Determined to promote the wearing of tartan, King George had been willingly persuaded to dress up, and spared no imagination, or expense in his theatrical attire.

He set foot in Edinburgh and promptly festooned himself in tartan. Proudly overclad in scarlet Stuart tartan jacket and kilt, with white and scarlet hose (some say underpinned by flesh pink silk hose – or tights) he elevated the wearing of tartan to heights of popularity still evident today.

But as to who wore the first tartan where and why, we shall probably never know.

GREEN MOURNERS

Giving credence to the theory that tartan was woven in certain areas in large quantities as an economy measure by the local chief, who then outfitted his men in matching dress purely on these prosaic grounds, is the tale of the Clan Sinclair.

Superstition dies hard in the Highlands, and the following is still remembered in Caithness.

At the Battle of Flodden a number of the Clan Sinclair crossed the River Ord on a Monday to join the Fray. The warriors were all dressed in green, and, almost to a man, they fell in defence to their king. For several generations afterwards no man of the name of Sinclair in Caithness would put on green, or cross the Ord on a Monday. If it was absolutely essential to cross on that day, the journey was performed by sea.

BONDAGERS

They may have been female farm labourers, almost serfs, indebted not to the farmer who owned the land, or even to his manager or factor, but to his hired male hand or 'hind'. However the dress of the bondager, picturesque, distinctive as a uniform and proudly worn was a common sight in the Border fields until the first World War.

A bondager was a woman who was 'bonded' or promised to work for a farmer. A farm male worker or 'hind' was taken on by a farmer, provided both himself and a bondager would labour for him. Frequently this woman bondager would have been his wife, but if not, he was obliged to find another woman to fulfil this part of the bargain. She would live with the hind and his family in a 'cotter' house, share their meals and help on the farm. Sometimes, the farmer would take on a 'hind' on the proviso that his wife also would help out at certain busy times, such as the harvest. Her work was payment for the rent of the tied house.

It was a strange custom, almost unknown elsewhere in the country, and no one knows just when or how it originated.

More puzzling still is the reason why such a lowly worker dressed in this self-imposed uniform, which was worn almost without change for generations. The women wore skirts of stout orange and black drugget (felted or coarse woollen fabric) with 'thirty eight pleats' according to one eye witness account. The binding of the hem, which fell below the knees, was a brightly coloured braid. Other accounts describe the skirt as being of sturdy grey material, and over it went an apron of striped red, blue, black and white fabric. The skirt was hitched up above the ankles, to keep it out of the mud of the farmyard, and on their feet the women wore sturdy boots.

But the most distinctive feature of this garb was the hat, usually made of varnished black straw, wide brimmed, perhaps lined in a bright cotton print, and held down by another square scarf which would be tied under her chin. Often she would wear a matching print blouse.

The bondager would need this wide shady hat both for protection from winds in the winter and sun during harvest time. The pretty costume which she wore, and in which most women took immense pride, appearing in clean clothes at the commencement of each day's toil, was all the more poignant for her drudgery which was far from genteel.

However decorative bondagers might have appeared in the sunlit fields at harvest time, they also needed to be strong and tough. Backbreaking work such as lifting turnips was followed by filthy jobs such as clearing out the muck from overwintered cattle in the byres. To protect her as much as possible from the worst of the dung or mud, she would bind her legs and arms with plaited ropes of straw. In wet weather she would lift up her outer skirts, bunching them around her waist and cover her petticoats with a thick canvas apron.

It was a harsh life. Because they held the purse strings, traditionally men escaped such jobs as dung clearing, defining it as 'women's work' and even after the birth of a baby, women bondagers were expected to be back working a day or so later in the fields, with their baby firmly wrapped to their back in a shawl.

At the two hiring fairs of the year, in March and September, women requiring work as bondagers would stand in the market place, dressed up proudly in their costumes and wait for a hind to come and bid for them. They stood amid others seeking employment, each displaying prominently the token of his trade. Grooms would clutch a riding whip, ploughboys a pitchfork, shepherds their crooks.

A bondager was well down the pecking order, almost a chattel, not even hired directly by the farmer. She would go with a hind after bartering her terms. She would have to agree to a bargain and then this would be sealed by the hind giving her 'arles' – a shilling. She was then committed until the next hiring day. She would hope that the hind would keep to his side of the bargain, that she would at least have a bed of her own, and not be required to share it with his children, or indeed himself, and that she would be fed and paid as promised.

Pawns within such a scheming workplace, they had but one path of defiance, their dress. With no home of their own, their dress became a mobile armoury against the world, and often wove its own clannish solidarity with others of their ilk. Many bondagers passed the tradition down to their daughters, frequently advising and protecting others as best they could from the worst of conditions and employers, and took pride in their work. A good bondager would expect a better than average pay, although it would always be less than a hind.

Pitted against odds which were generally well stacked against them, their defence was to dress proudly, prettily and cock a snoop against an unfair world.

GLOVERS

To modern eyes it is a curious sight, the Glovers costume of Perth. With its ankle length creamy coloured skirt, overlaid with a green bodice, and green pointed ribbons dangling down the sleeves at the shoulders it looks like a theatrical hand-me-down. Then there are the sleeves, with their bands of fabric supporting rows of bells and scarlet ribbons.

Add the headgear, with its strings dangling down almost to conceal the wearer, finished off with nut shells knotted at the ends. The shells themselves are a curiosity. They have been identified as probably Thevetia Peruviana, originally a native of central America and the West Indies, but introduced to cultivation about 1753.

The Glovers costume is the subject of great debate and interest, and can be seen in the Perth Museum and Art Gallery. Charles I visited Perth in the summer of 1633 and after listening to a sermon was conducted to his host's garden, overlooking the River Tay to watch an entertainment, riskily taking place on a floating platform on the fast flowing water.

The Glovers performed a dance on this platform, a challenging event, as it culminated in a sword dance. They left a detailed description of this in their minutes, not surprising in view of the amount they had spent on this entertainment, which amounted to 350 merks, £233 13s 4d (Scots) or £20 sterling. The performance was a flamboyant affair, culminating in a human pyramid, with others weaving and dancing round about, and ending up with wine glasses being flung to the ground in celebration.

> 'his Majesty's chair being set upon the wall next the Water of Tay whereupon was a floating stage of timber clad about with birks, upon the which for his Majesty's welcome and entry thirteen of our brethren of this our calling of glovers with green caps, silver strings, red ribbons, white shoes and bells about their legs, shearing rapiers in their hands and all other abulzement danced our sword dance with many difficult knots and allapallajesse, five being under and five above upon their shoulders, three more dancing through their feet and about them drinking wine and breaking glasses. Which (God be praised) was acted and done without hurt or skaith to any.'

Although the costume has been altered over the centuries, several curious anomalies occur. How did the group perform such an athletic gymnastic dance in ground length skirts, and from where did the idea for this costume and performance come? Well, the more energetic dancers seemed to be wearing similar costumes, but shortened versions, above the knees, quite likely leaving others in ground-length garb the ones who danced around this team. The sword dance was more likely to have been a version of the hilt and sword dance, a less energetic affair than the version common at today's Highland Games. But the origins of the costume, from where the inspiration came, and the proud guarding of this unique surviving garment for all these centuries poses more questions than answers. And why would a group such as the Glovers possess such a dress?

Considerably more knowledge relates to the Glovers themselves, a group who enjoyed much prestige in the town. The Perth Glovers during the 18th century were nationally acclaimed for the volume and standard of their work.

'Old Baillie Gray alone had seventeen men cutting gloves to keep his sewers in work, his son Robert for many years carried on a considerable trade after his father's death... numerous hands were employed in the cutting department, and a vast number of women earned a comfortable living by sewing them.'

So reported Penny in his *Traditions of Perth* published in 1880.

The glovers were rich and powerful in the town by the 1600s, owning large tracts of land in and around Perth. During their heyday by the end of the 1700s they were producing 20,000 to 30,000 pairs of gloves each year, and were taking a major part in all aspects of the town life. Even today, the incorporation meets twice a year, the head is still called the deacon and membership is still a heredi-tary right passed from father to son.

In addition to making gloves and buckskin breeches, the glovers also turned their skills to sheep and goat skins, which were sent to the London market for the covering of saddles and making of knap-sacks.

Much wealth was generated from the entire business, a motto which was carved into the side of one house owned by a glover:

'Wha would have thought it, that skins would have bought it.'

The glovers were clearly an amusing bunch, much given to dancing, jollity and operating a tight closed shop.

In the 18th century, tight buckskin breeches (known at the time as tights) were all the rage for men. Their making was an art apparently fine-tuned by one glover, who was 'equally distinguished for being a knight of the trencher.'

This bucolic gentleman had been commissioned to make a pair of buckskin breeches for a dashing officer belonging to the cavalry which was then stationed in Perth.

The officer was heard by the landlord at the George Inn (still in business in George Street in Perth) complaining bitterly that his breeches were too tight a fit and that he would make the glover eat them if he had the power, to which the jolly innkeeper observed that the glover was well known for his overindulgence of the bottle and his gourmandising.

Some days later, the glover was invited up to receive his money, and complimented by the officer on the tight finish of the breeches. Perhaps he would like to partake in a meal at the Inn? The innkeeper, on being asked with what delicacies he could entertain his guest, replied that his cook had just prepared a dish of finest tripe in a quite new recipe.

Tucking in with a will to his dish of tripe washed down with brandy, the glover rose to thank his guest and take his leave, at which point he was told that he was particularly fortunate, 'as he had his money in his pocket and the buckskins in his belly' a tale which lost nothing in the telling to fellow officers and glove makers.

SCARLET GOWNS OF A UNIVERSITY

Where would postcard manufacturers be without a splash of colour to liven up the grey Scots winter? St Andrews may have more than its share of historic buildings and traditions, but none so engrosses the amateur and professional snappers than the sight of a procession of red gowned students parading down the pier on Sundays. The procession always takes place after the church service finishes – harking back to days when the visiting presbytery arrived by boat, and the student faithful would escort him politely back down to his vessel, and wish him a safe journey.

The wearing of red gowns is a tradition which goes back to medieval times, although one wonders about the density of scarlet then. It was much later, on the banks of the Clyde in the late 1700s, that the dye Turkey Red raised the colour of textiles in one fell swoop. However, the gowns worn by students were some hue of red, and a good contrast they must have been to the drab browns and sludge tones worn by the local populace.

It was for precisely this reason that the scarlet gowns had to be worn. Tradition states that the students were thus clad to make them immediately conspicuous if attempting to enter a brothel. Divinity students, then and now clad in deep black, were deemed above suspicion. Further, the scarlet robes would render the wearer immediately distinguishable from the local ruffians, with whom they were in frequent physical disagreement. (*Praeco*, the alternative St Andrews student prospectus assures readers that this custom is now extinct.)

The style in which the gown is worn is a tradition in itself. First year students are called bejants/bejantines, from the French 'bec-jaune' or yellowbill, in other words those who are still naive, green, wet behind the ears. First years wear their gowns on both shoulders. After this, it is a yearly downward slump. Second years wear them just slipped back off the shoulders, third years fully expose one shoulder, and fourth years and longer inmates sweep and drag them about in their wake.

PAISLEY PATTERNS

All over the world, people recognise the pattern as 'Paisley', although most are baffled by which country, and where in that country such a place called Paisley is located.

The Paisley patterned shawl is a development of an Indian Kashmiri shawl, which was originally woven on a simple hand frame loom. Various names have been given to the pattern, for instance 'teardrop' or pine cone.

Valerie Reilly, keeper of Local History and Textiles at Paisley Museum is a leading expert in the evolution of the pattern, and explains that the origins of the motif can be found in the ancient civilisation of Babylon under the rule of Kings such as Nebuchadnezzar. There one of the predominant food sources was the date palm, which not only provided food but was the all encompassing base for life. From the palm tree came shelter, as well as wood, string and thatch. The coiled up frond of the embryonic date palm is the recognisable shape still seen today in Paisley pattern.

Therefore this symbol became significant and associated with the very beginnings of life.

From the hot dry land in the Middle East to the mills of damp, temperate Paisley on the west coast of Scotland is a lengthy travelling tale, with a few hints of commercial skulduggery, amusement, a military and staunchly Royal connection.

The pattern is known to have appeared again in India around the 17th century. This pattern was used on the very elaborate and valuable shawls being made from this time onwards, woven with wool gathered from a species of wild goat, the downy fleece of which, grown to protect it from the extreme chill of the Himalayan winter, was snagged onto bushes during the moulting period in the warmer spring. So soft and fine was this wool, and woven into such elaborate shawls which might have taken skilled weavers at least a year to manufacture, that the shawls were worn only by the wealthiest men in the area. Highly prized, they were exchanged as presents between princes.

Into this decorative world arrived the enterprising and bold employees of the British East India company, as well as regiments of British soldiers, who bought shawls as presents for the womenfolk back home. Exotic, brilliantly patterned, a touch of mystique to the pattern and, most important of all, different, shawls became a desirable acquisition. From this point on, it was but a series of steps before someone decided to manufacture copies in Britain.

By 1784 Norwich followed Edinburgh's lead in 1777 in weaving these shawls. But in Paisley, the skilled weavers concentrated on silk, and were fully occupied. The military ambitions of Napoleon quite suddenly brought their busy lives to a halt. The French wars meant that all British ships were zigzagging the French blockade to bring in essential supplies, and silk was certainly not a top priority.

Into this international crisis walked an Edinburgh shawl manufacturer called Mr Patterson, who around 1805 had taken on too many orders. Hearing of the available labour in Paisley, he sent some off to be made up, and from this beginning, the weavers of Paisley rapidly built themselves a reputation as excellent manufacturers and wended the Paisley name into a pattern which had meandered across the world.

That the enterprising men from Paisley grabbed such a challenge and cornered the market comes as no surprise when learning more of their character.

Not only did the weavers exchange knowledge and information about looms, weaving and possibly improvements, they were also interested in politics, and loomshops contributed to a fund enabling them to share a weekly newspaper and keep up with world events. Some were poets, such as Robert Tannahill who was a Paisley weaver – and they founded one of the earliest Horticultural Societies in 1792.

Into their designs crept personal touches. One shawl design incorporates carnations, one of the flowers much cultivated by the weavers.

Into their business also marched enterprise. Black centred shawls were woven in 1819 upon the death of Queen Charlotte, and white centred ones became a general inclusion for a bride's trousseau. She would wear this after the birth of a child. Little wonder then, that these white centred ones have been passed down the generations in families, although now it is the baby which is wrapped into the shawl for the christening.

When the fashion for shawls suffered from a slump in the 1840s, forcing 500 weavers to become the first assisted immigrants to arrive in Auckland in 1842, Queen Victoria heard of their plight and publicly wore her shawls, thereby instantly restoring their popularity.

The original imported shawls had been woven from the fleece of the special type of Central Asian wild goat, using the best underfleece shed in the summer. This underfleece was grown from protection during the extremely cold winters and the best fleece came from the goats living in the highest and therefore coldest areas.

Valerie Reilly describes how, among several attempts made to naturalise these goats in Great Britain, a vet called William Moorcroft brought back 50 from an expedition to Tibet. Unfortunately, the very careful family planning resulted in the females and males sailing in separate ships, and the project was abruptly terminated when the ship carrying all the females sank.

The pattern though, is firmly entrenched with the name of Paisley.

FAIR ISLE

Any island named the Fair Isle inspires romance. Tucked away north of Orkney, its green high cliffed shape appears as though dropped in mistake by a large mystical hand amid a wild sea.

The reality of life on the Fair Isle was and is very harsh. Fishing, farming and survival. The sheep provided an essential facet to life, and the wool became equally synonymous. While many designs might have evolved over centuries, the distinctive Fair Isle pattern, also recognisable the world over, quite suddenly burst upon an appreciative world – at least that is the popular image. No one truly knows.

The distinctive OXO effect is variously attributed to the Moorish influence, ancient Celtic patterns, Spanish or Baltic.

Tempting as it is to connect the Fair Isle pattern with a Moorish cross, there is no definite evidence to support such a claim. Some suggestions have pointed to the patterns being copied from knitted clothes worn by drowned Spanish sailors. Knowing the close links between Spain and the North African countries, this idea is not as far fetched as it sounds, but this theory falters in view of further evidence.

AND THE BALTIC?

Alice Starmore, a noted knitting expert who lives on the Isle of Lewis and has written copiously about the origins of pattern, is convinced that the most likely theory of the origin of the famous

Fair Isle pattern emerges from the Baltic region.

The Fair Isle was a regular port of call from ships coming from these areas, and an 1850 silk hat and woollen cap and pouch probably came from Finland and Estonia. Perhaps one of the women of Fair Isle, skilled and keen knitters, saw an exciting new method of pattern making and attracted to the bright colours and something new and exciting, decided to copy this sophisticated piece of work. She then developed this relatively simple pattern, which it still remains, into the distinctive and famous 'look' which has been credited with Fair Isle for a hundred years. Generations of children have been dressed in jumpers of these designs, and the patterns have evolved into modern day classics.

It was not always so. Like many a 'classic' look, this did not arrive by accident but by a shrewd manipulative move from a Lerwick draper by the name of James A. Smith in 1921. He presented the then Prince of Wales, who was already noted for setting fashion trends, with a Fair Isle knitted jumper. Clad in his present, the Prince of Wales conveniently posed for his portrait for the St Andrews Golf Club, and in one bound Fair Isle became a noted pattern all over the world.

SHETLAND ISLAND DANCING SHOES

Until the building of public halls during the latter part of the 19th century, most dances took place either out of doors or in barns when they were cleared out at the end of the winter. Men wore their Sunday boots for dancing – patent dancing shoes were not worn until much later – and the women wore shoes with a small heel. But in Shetland they wore special 'tatted socks' which were socks with thicker and stronger soles worked into them by the knitter. A keen dancer could pride herself on the number of 'tatted socks' which she wore out during the festive times, either during a wedding or at Christmas.

AND SHETLAND ISLAND GUISERS

'In walks a tall, slender looking man, called the scuddler, his face closely veiled with a white cambric napkin and on his head a cap made of straw, in shape like a sugar loaf, ie conical with three loops at the upper extremity, filled with ribbons of every conceivable hue, and hanging down so as nearly to cover the cap. He wears a white shirt, with a band of ribbons around each arm and a bunch of ribbons on each shoulder with a petticoat of long clean straw, called gloy, which hangs loosely.'

Although commonly associated with Hallowe'en, in Shetland men called Guisers would appear at a wedding, their leader being entitled the scuddler. In Delting he carried a broom and endeavoured to sweep everything in the room to the bride. On occasions, in his enthusiasm, he even swept the dirt from outside the house in to her.

The remaining Guisers were known as 'skeklers', dressed in a similar manner, but were meant to represent certain characters. In some other islands they each danced a short solo as they entered, but in Shetland they danced a Shetland Reel known as the Guisards Reel, and had a special tune of their own. After this, they joined in the general dancing for a while, always without speaking a word, least they disclose their identity.

RIVER PEARLS

There it sits, Little Willie, in a place of honour within the shop.

Smooth, the size of small thumb and gleaming milky white. Its worth a cool £60,000. No wonder then that this unexpected pearl was the subject of a much fought court case. The pearl sits in the Cairncross shop, a convivial Perth jeweller's shop with the Asprey touch in the best street of this proud little town. It was plucked from the Tay by Bill Abernethy (hence Willie's pearl) in 1967 and has been on display there since that year. Cairncross also buy all other Scottish pearls, and are almost alone in so doing.

Scottish pearls are a rarity today, found by a raggletaggle band of fishermen, whose strange apparatus is little changed today from

Roman or Medieval times, give or take the addition of thermal underwear and rubber waders. Today's fishermen are culled from 'travellers', those in favour of a nomadic life, those not too concerned with a fat bank account, and one outstanding character, Bill Abernethy, whose knowledge is by all accounts encyclopedic. Early descriptions of pearl fishers show them shuffling with bare feet in the water, feeling for mussels to open in search of the treasure.

Roman historian Suetonius described Caesar weighing up a handful of British pearls, and suggesting that the invasion of Britain was prompted by his desire for such riches. In any event, Caesar was prompted to donate a breastplate studded with pearls to a goddess Venus Genetrix.

Even before Mary Queen of Scots wore Scottish pearls in the 16th century, Alexander I wore a Scots pearl in 1120, Robert the Bruce's crown was decorated with one, and James V had the largest ever set into his sceptre.

Henry V apparently had one stolen from his tent during the Battle of Agincourt. Mention was made of Scots pearls in a statue of goldsmiths of Paris in 1355. Scottish pearls decorate both English and Scots regalia. Queen Victoria was a proud owner, as was Edward VII, and most modern British Royal ladies possess Tay pearls.

The pearls' appeal and desirability reached a zenith in Paris in the 17th century, when the Rue Lafayette was the pivot of the pearl industry. Not that it was admitted that they came from Scotland. To add gloss to their milky allure, they were renamed 'oriental' – presumably conjuring up a more romantic view than shivering near-naked fishermen delving for the prize in a rain sodden Scotland.

Cold and shivery work it may be, especially as the best time to fish is when the first frosts have killed off the vegetation, but the name 'pearlers' conjures up an attractively alternate way of life.

Although most pearlers come from 'travelling' stock, there is an aura of mystery surrounding others. They were misty, silent characters, who were just known as Pearly Johnny or Newburgh Jock.

Knowing where to look and grasp the pearls was a fund of historic knowledge passed down the family line. Pearl fishers continue searching to this day, but are far from easy to locate. A strange, secretive little band, they are almost as invisible as the pearls for which they search.

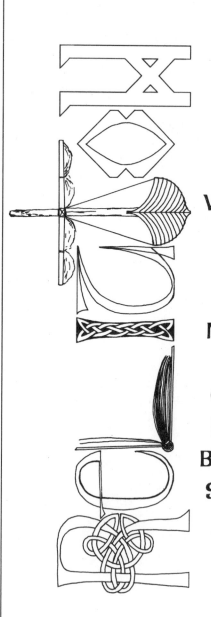

Floating Islands and Waterborne Churches, Mythical Saints, Modern Day Pilgrims. Of Heather Priests and Bell, Book and Shinty Stick.

FLOATING ISLAND ON THE WITCHES LOCH

Dava Loch might not be the most insignificant loch in Scotland, but it is a strong contender. The very ordinary looking expanse of water is set into one end of a peat bog, and allegedly never runs dry. Locally it was known as the Witches Loch, and its dark and peaty appearance do not belie the name.

Sir Thomas Dick Lauder, who wrote many books about the legends and fairy stories of the Highlands in the 1800s, tells the tale in his *Highland Legends*. It is a tale of intrigue, unrequited love, witches, water, fairies and a happy ending well worth reaching...

The story centres around Mary Rose, who was the daughter of a successful local farmer, and her love for Robin Stuart, who was but a mere ploughboy. Father Donald Rose did not of course approve of this match, as not only had he come up in the world, but was he himself not also 'come o' a cousin sax times removed of the Laird of Kilravock himself?' He was adamant, Mary was not to meet Robin Stuart.

But Father Rose was not around all the time, it seemed, and, happily, he was clearly not the type to lock up his daughter. So when Father Rose set off for the day to a market, Donald and Mary spent the day together, and wandered near to the Dava Loch.

When they reached the Witches Loch, Mary pointed out the little island, but a yard from the edge of the water, which had upon it a post draped with weeds and rags, and telling Donald in jest that this was the Fairy Island, leapt out and landed there. Donald jumped on with her, and to their astonishment, realised that the island was floating away to the midst of the loch, and they were surrounded by uninviting, sinister, dark, peaty water, which looked all of a sudden extremely well-named as the Witches Loch.

So there they were, marooned in the midst of the loch for hours, and as the sun went down, worse seemed about to happen. It grew colder, and Donald wrapped his plaid round the pair of them. It then dawned upon them that their little island was slowly sinking.

Mary, thinking that this was their last hour, prayed that they might be saved from this fate. Promptly of course, a wind then sprung up. Donald, proving that he was quick witted as well as having a strong sense of self preservation, held the plaid above his head, and the island with its marooned passengers floated gently back to the shore. No sooner were they nearly there, than they heard the clear sounds of Father Rose's horse trotting close by on the path. There was nowhere to hide, and no possible way of avoiding detection. Mary screamed and they both flung themselves down on the ground, but when they cautiously reared up to see what reaction Father Rose was to have, their eyes only met the moor, and the sound of stampeding hooves galloping away.

Donald Rose galloped through the night, terrified and traumatised by the sight which had just met his eyes. Maybe he had imbibed too readily at the market, but there was no escape from the realisation of what he had just seen, 'twa speerits' like wraiths, speeding over the water towards him 'far faster than ony wild duke (duck) could flee.' He plunged on through the night, caught up in the boggy ground and careering this way and that until he at last reached his home.

There was his daughter Mary with Robin and his father, exhausted and muddy, having staggered home via a short cut across the moor, arriving before Mary's father. Never was a father so glad to see his family and never did he ever want to see such a thing again. Sir Thomas Dick Lauder does not tell us precisely why Father Rose changed his mind about his daughter's affections. Perhaps he recognised a man who 'saved' his daughter from the evil spirits on the loch was a man to respect. Who knows. Certainly, Mary Rose and Robin Stuart never revealed the true existence of the flying devils on the island in the loch, and lived happily ever after.

As for the Witches Loch and the floating island. It was certainly still floating about at the end of the 1940s, when the story was retold in the *Scots Magazine*, and Sir Thomas suspected that it was merely a chunk of peat which was broken off by wind and flood. If so, there can be few stories which end so happily and few chunks of peat which have floated so romantically into legend.

THE GREEN ISLE

When St Finan sailed over to the west coast of Scotland from Ireland in his coracle, he sailed right up to Kilchoan, on the Ardnamurchan point. Then he abandoned his coracle and walked on over the hills. Although his faith was strong and his hopes high for the spreading of Christian knowledge in this heathen land, little was he to know that many centuries later, religious faith would still be taken to the people with awesome difficulty.

As he wandered by the shore of Loch Sunart, should he have been able to skip on through the centuries to 1846, he would have seen the 'floating church' of Strontian, a boat moored just out from the village. Upon this deck the gathering inhabitants would meet to hear the words of their Free Church minister. Forbidden by the local laird to build a church on his land, the congregation moored a boat as a floating church, outside the ownership or jurisdiction of any landowner. Each Sunday services were held on board, and tradition states that the most successful preachers would be judged by the numbers of parishioners they attracted. The measurement for this success was judged by how low the boat lay weighted in water.

As St Finan and his followers had then turned north and east, over from Loch Sunart to the long slender stretch of water of Loch Shiel, they would have been tramping the paths used in the future for the 'heather priests' of the 18th and 19th centuries. These Roman Catholic priests ministered to their receding flock on the west coast of Scotland. They searched out isolated followers, and leaving their seminary at Morar, would thereafter have no fixed abode. They would arrive in a community on foot, having traversed the hills and stayed at one of the houses occupied by a staunch Catholic. These priests were few and far between and their wanderings on foot to the most remote of hamlets meant that a visit from a priest was a rare and special occurrence for people whose belief had left them bereft of a permanent priestly presence. In the wave of Protestantism, the Roman Catholic followers were left squeezed out in the west. Pockets of Roman Catholic faithful occupy many outlying spots, where the advent of fierce and uncompromising Free Church leaders never made much impact. A visit to these communities by these lonely self-sufficient young Roman Catholic priests was greeted with joy, and babies, often born a considerable time previously would be thankfully baptised and blessed.

What thoughts might have gone through St Finan if he had but known that thousands of years later, religious beliefs would still be practised with such fear, determination and fervour. Ironically, he might well have found much comfort if he could have foreseen the tolerance with which both beliefs treated 'his' isle.

When St Finan dropped down to the shores of Loch Shiel, he spotted an island, regarding it as a safe haven upon which he settled. This became known as the Green Isle, Eilean Fhionain, or St Finan's Isle, situated but a few hundred yards from the north shore, nearer the Glenfinnan end.

Upon this island there was built a chapel, and much later, in the 16th century or thereabouts a burial ground was laid out by Allan, Chief of the Clanranald, while on the stone altar of the ruined chapel there was placed a bronze, Celtic handbell, no more than a hand high, known as the St Finan's Bell. Up until the turn of the 19th century, this handbell was brought down to the landing stage when a funeral party arrived, and solemnly rung by the leader of the procession as they wound their way up to the graveyard. Into this ground came many to be buried, and the irony of it is that the occupants were Catholic and Protestant, united in death and lying peacefully side by side.

THE SELF BUILT ISLAND BY SKAILL, ORKNEY

Skaill mansion house on the island of Orkney is one of the oldest continuously inhabited houses in Orkney and lays claim to one of the most poignant ghosts.

Legend relates how the loch, which stands opposite the house, set alight a wistful and single-minded ambition in one small boy. So determined was he to build his own island, that he rowed day after day to the centre of the loch with piles of stones, in order to construct his very own small piece of land. Finally, he carried sufficient quantities to make his island rise up above water level. He then stepped out of his rowing boat onto the hump, sat down, and promptly died. His ghost haunts the mansion house of Skaill.

THE WATERY FOUNDATIONS OF ST VIGEONS, FORFAR

The 11th century church at St Vigeons is today noted primarily for its remarkable collection of inscribed Celtic stones, carrying Pictish symbols. But in keeping with the misty overlap of Pagan and Christian beliefs, strong local tradition maintained that the materials for the building were carried by water kelpies – magic elves or fairies – and foundations laid on large bars of iron. Underneath this raft-like structure, and safely hidden from modern prying eyes, was supposed to be a deep lake.

Local tradition went further in prophesying two future events: that an incumbent of the church would commit suicide and that on the occasion of the first communion to be held after this sad event, the whole church would sink into the lake.

The first foretelling came about with a suicide in the early 1700s, and so strong was local feeling about the church sinking, that the congregation refused to countenance a communion service being held.

Finally, a service was held in 1736, and numerous local inhabitants took up their stance on a hill opposite, to watch what might happen. In the event, the church still stands, but the doubters have long since passed away.

HOW DULL ACQUIRED ITS NAME

The tiny ancient hamlet of Dull, near Aberfeldy in Tayside is uniquely, and to modern ears, rather quaintly christened. The naming was in honour of St Adamnan, who had been a disciple of Columba at the Monastery in Iona until he came over to the mainland of Scotland with St Fillan.

They had journeyed together until they reached Tyndrum where they stopped for the night and drew lots. Fillan drew the lot to stay where he was in Glenochart and Adamnan continued eastwards into Glenlyon. He stopped his travelling near the present Bridge of Balgie, settled there and soon built a mill. The place was called Milton Eonan, the Mill Town of Adamnan and from there Adamnan spread the Gospel up and down the Glen. His impact on the people of Glenlyon was enormous and his legend has descended over fourteen centuries. Local folk believed absolutely in his holy powers and when threatened by disaster they turned to Adamnan with implicit faith for deliverance.

A terrible plague swept through Scotland in the 17th century. It reached the Vale of Fortingall and so violent was its ravages that all the inhabitants were wiped out. Slowly the sickness began to infiltrate the Glen and in a panic the people of Glenlyon went to their preacher and beseeched him, 'Eonan of the ruddy cheeks, rise and check the plague of thy people. Save us from the death and let it not come upon us east or west...'

Adamnan rose to the occasion and gathered the people of the Glen to a hillock where he usually preached to them. In a house not forty yards away it is said that a child was already dying of 'the Death'.

There on the rock, with the people gathered round him, Adamnan prayed. When he was finished he raised his right arm, exhorted the devil body of the pestilence to come to him and pointing to a large round rock lying on the ground, ordered the plague to enter it. A large circular hole appeared in the rock as the plague bored into it and Adamnan followed up this apparent miracle by the very sensible act of sending all the healthy people of the Glen up to the shielings until all signs of pestilence disappeared. He himself stayed down in the Glen and nursed the sick.

Thus were the people of the Glen saved from the Plague. When they came back from their mountain retreat they erected a stone slab with two crosses on it to commemorate their deliverance. The rock itself is called the Craig-diannaidh, the 'rock of safety' and the round stone with the hole through which the plague descended into the bowels of the earth lies to this day at the side of the road near the stone slab.

Adamnan died in 704 A.D. He requested that his body be carried down the Glen on a stretcher and when the ties of the stretcher were so chafed they finally broke, there he was to be buried and a church and place of learning be erected in his name. His wish was carried out and his body borne down the Glen before a throng of mourners.

The first tie or 'dull' broke at Tulli and there, as he had requested, he was buried. But at Tulli there already existed a place of learning, a church and a sanctuary at which Adamnan had preached regularly. So a more fitting place for his burial would have been hard to find and the name was changed from Tulli to Dull, and the church and a fair held on his Saint's day were dedicated to his name.

ST MUNGO AND THE DOUBLE TIDES OF THE FIRTH OF FORTH

Between Culross and Alloa on the Firth of Forth, there are twice as many tides as normal. When the tide is flowing, and has done so for three hours, it recedes for the space of two feet, then returns to its normal course till it has reached the limit of high water. Similarly, in ebbing it begins to flow again and then recede to the limit of low water.

This strange occurrence is due entirely to St Mungo.

When the saint and some of his holy associates were sailing up the Forth to Stirling, their vessel went aground in ebb tide, and could not be floated. The saint immediately invoked his miraculous powers and the tide in consequence returned, therefore enabling his boat to proceed on their journey and there has been a double tide ever since in this area of the Forth.

THE ROBUST MINISTEIR MOR OF LAGGAN, INVERNESS

When the Roman Catholic church packed off the Reverend Duncan Macpherson to take charge of his parish in 1747, it was an outlying area which was little affected by the advent of Protestantism. It was of small surprise to the new arrival that the rigorous obeying of the Sabbath was not intensely observed. When he repaired to the rough little church with its thatched roof on the first Sunday to conduct the service, he noted that there was an energetic game of shinty in full swing down on the haugh by the riverside. (Shinty is a game similar to hockey, played with great flourish by the northern Scots and Irish. The rules are less onerous than traditional hockey.)

Boldly the new minister requested the players to accompany him to church, to which the players promised to listen to his sermon if he would take a caman or club and play with them first. Rising to this challenge, he strode off to the ground, and played with such vigour that the clubs were piled up at the door and his impressed team mates trooped in his wake.

It was a sharp test of what was to come, although it is related that he prayed with much fervour against the sin of Sabbath breaking and especially with regard to the part which he had been compelled to play. But it was all justified to 'win a stiff necked and rebellious people from the error of their ways'.

Nicknamed by his parishioners Ministeir Mor on account of his Herculean build, he proved to hold not only a deep sense of his calling but also a marked ability to adapt to whatever fate and circumstances dictated.

He lived on one side of the River Spey, while the church and most of his parishioners occupied the other. There was no bridge, and frequently the spates of late winter were an insurmountable obstacle – well, for anyone by Ministeir Mor.

Directing the faithful from both sides to a quieter part of the river, the Minister would stand on a boulder, and preach his sermon.

His fine touch of the practical was probably due to the exigencies of a parish such as Laggan. If the banns of marriage had to be proclaimed, he would demand that the fee would be wrapped in a piece of cloth, and thrown across the river before he made the announcement. And it is said that if the money fell short and into the water, the thrower was to stand the loss.

Like the heather priests of the west coast, who had no permanent home, but wandered from hamlet to hamlet over the hills ministering to the faithful, one of the main tasks was to baptise he many new and fragile infants who arrived.

When the Spey was impassable, he would signal over to the father to bring the child to the point on the opposite bank where the water was contracted and rushed through like a swollen mill race. Then with a great sweep of his arm, he used to throw across some water, which the father would watch anxiously in its flight, and try and bring the baby within range. Several attempts were often required, but tradition states that the minister never failed altogether. Then, for the rest of the service, he would direct the participants down the water to a calmer spot.

A legend in its own lifetime was the great figure of Ministeir Mor, and for many years tales of his life travelled round about. Sadly, he was only at Laggan for but ten years, before he was smitten by pneumonia and died.

RABELLICK'S BURIAL GROUND

The anxiety to have babies baptised was of small surprise, given that children who died before being blessed were buried in unconsecrated grounds, usually well outside the places of habitation.

All over the Highlands and Islands there were impromptu gravesites, usually unmarked, and often containing not only unbaptised children, but suicides, murderers and those unknown locally.

At the tip of Glen Lyon is the flat moot hill called Sithean Tom na Cloin – the childrens' Fairy Hill – where until the middle of the 19th century, unbaptised babies were buried during hours of darkness, and left for the fairies to spirit away.

Another such place is on a featureless knoll about a mile above Crathie on the Markie River, near Newtonmore, and it was known by the name of Rabellick. Before it became this last resting place for unbaptised children, the last known burial was that of a soldier in the wars of Montrose. His body was carried over the hills from the Great Glen and down the Markie River to this place. There were no able-bodied men left in the country to act as bearers, but one, a tailor. The rest of the mourners were women and there the women and the tailor dug the grave and buried the man.

Thereafter it was used just for babies, in accordance with a harsh religious doctrine of the time, 'which barred the gates of Heaven with a curse against all infants who died without baptism or minister.' So when the people of Crathie fell out, their favourite curse was the hurl at the accused 'may you be buried in Rabellick'.

PROTECTION FOR MOTHERS OF UNCHRISTENED BABIES

Such was the fear for children dying unbaptised, and the effect this would have on the mother, that great precautions were taken to offer protection: either a row of nails driven into the first board of the bed, or a smoothing iron or reaping hook placed under the bed. Finally, a father's shirt was wrapped round the baby or the mother's wedding dress spread over it.

A DAY IN MAY

'Pilgrimage is a day out with a purpose. After all, all that crusading in the Holy Land was an aspect of primitive tourism laced with a mixture of religion and military adventure,' observed columnist Patrick O'Donavon.

His namesake, Patrick, Earl of Lauderdale, would wholeheart-edly agree. For it was to the yearly May pilgrimage to Haddington, twelve miles east of Edinburgh, and organised by the Earl, to which Patrick O'Donavon was referring.

The ecumenical service takes place within a building which was finally completely resorted in 1976, and attracts followers from all corners of Scotland and beyond; catchment perimeters to date extend from the Isle of Skye to Durham.

Lord Lauderdale enthuses about the 'favours' pilgrims have been rewarded with. How the architect, puzzling about how to reconstruct the vanished, vaulted roof, suddenly feeling that someone was standing behind him, turned round, and presently saw a carved stone, the vital clue he needed.

Other stories bear their own witness. The Earl's grandson, brain damaged at birth and now near normal. The alcoholic man who managed to make a U-turn and re-found his wife. In 1972 no more than thirty attended the service; nearly twenty years on, that has grown to thousands.

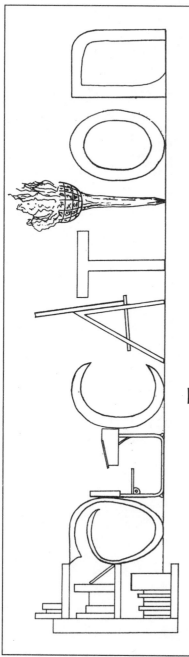

From Cradles of Stone to Eminent Institutions. Isolated Islands as Lairs for Pictish Powerhouses and a Thraldom for an Awkward Lady.

EDUCATION AND CHARACTER

In that elusive mix of character which makes the Scots into the characters they are, education shines as a leading navigational light through the centuries. Long before such elevation through learning alone was common in Europe, Scots from farm, glen and fishing backgrounds rose from humble origins through the widespread education.

Perhaps it was rooted in the great storytellers of Celtic and Pictish myths, when long dark winter evenings gave vent to tales of mystery and intrigue. Added to this was a vibrant mixture of invaders, who by the very nature of their courage must have been the most outstanding people of their race. When they settled in the land, they added dimensions of knowledge and culture. Then the influence of religion from the earliest days of the great saints promoted learning as an end in itself.

Scots education transcended class and was valued for its own sake. The 'lad o' pairts' was encouraged by teacher and frequently found a place at University. Indeed, the story of Scots University education commenced early.

Towards the end of the 16th century, while England had two Universities established, Oxford and Cambridge, there were already four in Scotland. In the dying years of this 16th century, an even more astonishing educational fact emerged. Aberdeenshire possessed three Universities, Kings College in Old Aberdeen, founded in 1494, Marischal College in the 'New Town' of Aberdeen, founded in 1593, and preceding this by one year, the University of Fraserburgh.

The University of Fraserburgh was founded by Sir Alexander Fraser, the Laird of Philorth, described as a 'piouse and learned gentleman of that neighbourhood,' and his aims were in tune with the philanthropic desires of great local men of the time. He constructed a new harbour, church, public buildings and streets, and it was but a logical step to improve the facilities for learning within this proud new burgh.

There might have been a touch of rivalry between Sir Alexander Fraser and his neighbour at Peterhead, George, the fifth Earl of Marischal, who established the college named after him at Aberdeen. However, competition or not, the beneficiaries were the future scholars in the North East of Scotland.

Sir Alexander Fraser had to firstly win support for his proposal from the King, James VI, a monarch who favoured the promotion of learning. In the July of 1592, Sir Alexander was granted a deed enabling him not only to build a university, but to raise funds for the same, control the governors for such an institution and grant whatever more was needed and was within the royal power.

With such a mandate, the path appeared to have been cleared, but five long years later, on 16 December 1597, the Scottish Parliament passed an Act concerning the funding and support of the University of Fraserburgh, but recognised that such an under-taking as this might well be in need of greater funding and support than was possible for Sir Alexander to provide alone. By this time some building had taken place, and in the following year Mr Charles Ferme was appointed as Principal, his duties having to double with that of minister Philforth, a dual role which was common at the time.

The records of the University for this time are sparse and the most that probably happened was that Mr Ferme taught a limited number of students for a few years.

Sadly at some point during this time, the University was dealt a hard blow from which it never recovered. Mr Ferme was probably imprisoned, not for any impropriety, but because he defied the strong desire for episcopacy advocated by the King, who insisted on 'No bishop, No King,' and attending an assembly which was contra to an Act of 1584 against convoking ecclesiastical assemblies without the King's authority, was banished for several years, prob-ably from 1605 until 1609. He was more fortunate than many who were banished for life. He was sent either to the Castle of Tain or the Castle of Bute and then the Isle of Bute. P.J. Anderson, writing in his account of *The Aberdeen Universities at Peterhead and Fraserburgh* in 1887, describes how Mr Ferme was finally allowed to return to his cure, where he zealously discharged his duties, teaching both in public and in private, until 'worn out by study and shattered by incessant toil and sufferings, he died on September 24, 1617, aged 51.'

Financially, the University was also suffering. Sir Alexander's expenditure on the development of the town and University finally reduced him to debt, and he was forced to sell his Castle at Fraserburgh and much of his land.

That the University then faltered was also due to the lack of students, whom Sir Alexander had hoped would materialise from the Highlands and locally. The town itself was still fairly undeveloped, and those who would have come from further afield, then might have been just as well to proceed to Aberdeen, where there were by now two well established universities.

But there was a final twist to the tale. In 1647, a University did establish itself in Fraserburgh. The reason for this exodus was in order to avoid the plague, which had gradually swept up from Edinburgh, arriving in Aberdeen in June 1647.

In an effort to escape the consequences, both Universities in Aberdeen packed up and left. Marischal College, as befitting the home of its founder, migrated to Peterhead, while King's College from Old Aberdeen settled for a while in Fraserburgh, although solid written proof of this event is lacking. Only hearsay gives us a clue.

It must have been the last time that students occupied the town, but the fact that Sir Alexander Fraser bequeathed so much of his wealth to such an institution is in itself a fitting epitaph to the Scottish desire for learning.

Just over 200 years later, nothing had changed in the number of Universities in Scotland, which still numbered four.

On 4 June 1829, Mrs Elizabeth Crichton, widow of Dr James Crichton of Friars Carse, Dumfries, decided that under the terms of her husband's will, (he had died six years before) she would like to endow a college or University in Dumfries.

Dr Crichton had had a notable career, both in medicine and commerce, when he had been a member of the East India

Company and later became Physician to Governor General of India. During this time in India and also China he had amassed a considerable fortune, and upon his death decreed that any monies left after all his bequests had been fulfilled should be used for charitable purposes. The decision as to how this sum was to be spent was to be taken by his wife and Trustees.

Mrs Crichton was clearly a lady who was determined to take such a bequest seriously, and she was anxious that the 'charitable proposed should answer the benevolent intentions of her husband and do honour to his memory, and at the same time promote the interests of the public, especially amongst the humbler classes of the community.'

Accordingly, six years after her husband's death, when a lengthy dispute by his brother over the terms of the will had been overcome, Mrs Crichton took her grand plan to the Trustees. She wished to found a college of learning in memory of her husband, and she hoped that this establishment would become a University.

For four long years the plans were drawn to the attention of the great and good in the land, as well as to those in whose hands the granting of such a charter would rest. The etching of Mrs Crichton shows a woman with gentle face, and determination of bearing, but she finally had to admit defeat.

The account of the time dryly notes that there were 'difficulties with other Universities and the Treasury, and the opposition of Lord Brougham, the Lord Chancellor of that time.'

Mrs Crichton may have been blocked by the Establishment, but she swiftly turned her attentions elsewhere. She was clearly not a lady to espouse a fashionable clause, as in place of a University, Dumfries now possesses the Crichton Institution for Lunatics. Mrs Crichton was initially much derided for her scheme, but she was determined that this institution would be the best of its type. In the end, Dumfries never acquired the opportunity again to become home to a University, but the Institution became renown world wide for its treatment and research, and Mrs Crichton is remembered today for the boldness of her views.

NOTIONAL CURES

Pioneering discoveries in health was not just confined to the wealthy.

A flat gravestone marks the grave of John Williamson, who was born at Eshaness Shetland, about 1740, died on the island in 1803. He was a crofter, but one with such powers of logic and invention that he was christened Johnnie Notions by his neighbours, so thoughtful and distant did he frequently appear to them.

His story started and finished with smallpox. He was born during one epidemic and spent his spare time perfecting the cure for the disease. He had no medical training, and probably little enough schooling, and it is fairly certain that he never left the islands.

Smallpox was the scourge of the islands, carried there as it was by travellers from ships, and appeared to strike almost every twenty years from 1700 onwards with devastating consequences. So widespread was the disease during these periods that it was commonly called the 'mortal pox'.

To battle against this disease came Johnnie Notions. His method was simple enough. He inoculated the patient by levering a tiny portion of skin from the arm, carefully avoiding any bleeding, and inserted a tiny amount of serum. Then he covered up the wound carefully and placed a cabbage leaf over the arm. His success was remarkable. When the disease broke out in 1791, it had little detrimental effect on the population. A Dr Edmondston, the local doctor on the island, writes how he would have been sceptical had he not seen the effect of this inoculation for himself. Not only did Johnnie Notions devise and perfect his 'notion' from an animal which he had infected, watching carefully until he judged the animal had built up the maximum antibodies, he also learnt that his vaccine had to be immensely dilute – as opposed to medical knowledge of the day when more meant cure – to be effective.

He was also an accomplished shoemaker, tailor, carpenter, cutler, farmer and fisherman, according to contemporary description. It was only the year after his death that any advance in the idea of

Continued on page 105

CAPTIONS TO PLATES
FOLLOWING PAGE 96

Photographs are reproduced by kind permission of the Scottish
Ethnological Archive, National Museums of Scotland

1

Scots ministers of religion followed in an intrepid line of saints and martyrs. These early leaders must indeed have forged an inspirational, but formidable track to follow. Many ministers of the Church, having been rigorously educated in the great universities, were then cast out into the often inhospitable rural heartlands to care for their flock. The harsh surroundings in which they frequently found themselves must have required every ounce of their faith and resilience, as well as an inner faith of inestimable depth.

Many churchmen remained in these remote parishes for most of their lifetime. It was a far cry from the theory so carefully studied in Theological College, and also required a cast iron constitution, as shown in this photograph of the minister in Luskintyre, Harris in 1894. He stands amid his flock with head tied up in a bandage.

2

Dance was an intrinsic part of the Scottish soul, practised with frequency on every occasion which offered an excuse. This couple might have been accompanying a wedding group from an island marriage ceremony. Sometimes many of the guests would dance their way over the water, a custom re-enacted before my own eyes in 1992 aboard a ferry from the Island of Mull to Oban.

Other wedding dances traditionally took place on the shore, where the links would provide an ideal dancing platform, and were sometimes the only alternative before the construction of a village hall.

3

Pearlers were secretive souls, part of a travelling community, whose skills had been gained through generations traced back to Medieval times. To them alone were known the best places in rivers around the land from which to scoop the precious river mussels. Many Kings and Queens of Scotland would boast Scottish river pearls within their royal regalia and ownership, a custom carried on to the present day. The pearls are collected using the same methods unchanged over centuries, and their whereabouts meticulously guarded. Little changes amid such a tradition, and the location of this scene is unknown.

4

The great droving days when thousands of black cattle were led down from the lush highland and west coast pastures to the 'trysts' or markets of Crieff and Falkirk are remembered with nostalgia and romance. A drove road now conjures up a pastoral idyll. A tryst has become a word symbolising a romantic meeting. Scottish trysts were great gathering places where Highlander met Lowlander, and the bards, musicians and merrymakers attached themselves to the meeting. From what might have been simply a hard bitten exchange of goods evolved an occasion of music and fun, a typical Scottish method of bending an occasion to enjoyment.

5

To Scotland came many immigrants over the centuries, men of vision, brutality, humanity and those whose arrival by shipwreck was unintentional. Of such a mix was the varied Scots character born. Even in the early days of their arrival, each immigrant would set down his baggage of inherited artistic talent. Thus to these shores came men whose main task was to carve intricate Celtic designs upon some of the lands hardest stones, a gift which was to last for centuries.

6

The early Christian disciples who arrived with St Columba and shortly after were sainted. This ancient sanctuary cross amid a rugged scene captures all the remoteness and unknown future faced by such men. This early cross at Kilchoman, on the Isle of

Islay, off the west coast of Scotland, epitomises the struggle to establish Christianity within a hostile environment. It is a pointer to the success which was to arrive, established against formidable odds.

7, 8

Hunting the Guga (the great sea bird, Sula Bassana) has taken place for hundreds of years, where men risk much to land on the inhospitable, waterless rock island of Sula Sgeir. Why do they still come to catch, kill and pickle these birds with salt in this century? It is best understood as a tribal right, a link with the distant past, the essence of island lore, a challenge and spirit of adventure. It is also a private pilgrimage between island men and their heritage.

9

This photograph of Fair Isle men beside their boat predates the time when the classic knitted pattern known the world over as 'Fair Isle' sprung into prominence through a shrewd manipulative move. One James A. Smith, a Lerwick draper presented a jumper to the then Prince of Wales, who wore it for a portrait presented to the St Andrews Golf Club. In one bound, Fair Isle pattern became world famous. But from where came the origins of this pattern? Some conjectured the Moorish cross influence came from Spanish ship wrecked mariners, others from the Baltic. How this pattern might have arrived here is a story more intriguing than the complexity of the knitting itself.

10

Christianity and old pagan customs overlapped all over the country. While one of the great festivals, that of Beltane, has died, Halloween remains alive and much celebrated, with young 'guisers' knocking on doors. These children dressed up in straw costumes were photographed in the early part of the twentieth century on the island of Fetlar, Shetland.

11

The stone heart constructed out of pebbles decorates an old road near Strachur in Argyll. For reasons unknown or not understood, this point was the place chosen by travelling folk for their weddings. The long path of marriage commenced here, but no registers record the numbers, names or dates.

12

On Ness, Lewis, where this photograph was taken, as all over the western island, each day of the week had special associations.

Di-Rdaoin, the Gaelic for Thursday, was a lucky day for the birth of a calf or lamb, as well as for the cutting of hair or a beard. On Di-Haoine, or Friday, it was unlucky to count animals or to go near a fire.

13

This 'itinerant' camp is photographed near Hawick in the Borders, and the fire in the centre of this gathering is just about to be lit.

In Glen Clova, when there was a drab, windless, wet day, the wisps of damp cloud which hung above the trees were known locally as 'tinkie reeks' as they looked just like the thin wisps of smoke which used to be seen rising from a gipsy encampment such as this.

14

Graveyards were sometimes far from the church, but in a strategic location with a view far out to sea. Filled with rough stones, this one is at Dunrossnes parish, about 4 miles from Sandwick in the south of the Shetland islands.

But churches also were sometimes situated as though cast away on the edges of island beaches, keeping a sea eagle's view over water which looks calm here, but was filled with unpredictable tide rips, sudden squalls, whispering sea monsters and enchanted seal fairies.

15

This gipsy lady taking a rest near Tain around 1920 was one of the Scots travellers or gipsies. They were made up of a gaggle of the descendants of those routed at Culloden, wanted men who had left the glens to fight in the Jacobite cause and never dared to return home for fear of persecution. They came to speak a language called the Cant, which is composed of Gaelic, old Scots and English words, all slightly adapted in their pronunciation.

Gipsy women such as these were supposed to have second sight and distribute curses, some of which are known to have become true.

16

Charlie Faa Blythe was crowned King of the Gipsies in 1898, becoming King Charles II, in succession to his mother, Queen Esther. His coronation took place at Kirk Yetholm, which was the headquarters of the Scottish gipsies and where there was also their 'palace', a small house with lattice windows, still standing today.

1 ▲

2 ▼

3 ▲

4 ▼

5 ▲

6 ▼

11 ▲

12 ▼

13 ▲

14 ▼

15 ▲

16 ▼

Continued from page 91

inoculation arrived in medical circles, and twenty years later that the idea was initially adopted.

Why the uneducated Johnnie Notions in Shetland should have made such pioneering strides in such an important development has never been discovered.

READING FOR ALL

Acquiring knowledge was open to almost all. The Innerpeffray Library, near Crieff, is one of the oldest to be founded in Scotland, opening its doors in 1691. It is open to this day, where the main original valuable books lining the walls can be taken down, and contemplated by 20th century visitors.

The library was the brainchild of a member of the Drummond family, whose graves are in the adjoining chapel. This particular Drummond scorned the other most popular occupation of his day, namely fighting, in favour of rural tranquility and gifting the search for learning to all.

Although today the library stands at the end of a long track leading to a collection of buildings housing the library, chapel and old school house, it was at a busy crossroads in its heyday.

Contained within its register which details the books loaned, when and by whom, are details of the borrowers occupations. Clearly recorded are the details of entire families, who made a weekly or monthly visit. In the latter part of the 19th century and well into the 20th, the library subscribed to magazines, which were popular items for loan. Fathers would list their occupations such as blacksmith, overseer, gamekeeper, clerk, park keeper, gardener, stationmaster, as well as scholar and divinity student.

The Library started to lose customers when the public libraries opened in 1919, and there was a sharp decrease in borrowings. Finally, Innerpeffray Library, now in its out of the way location and in competition with libraries positioned in towns round about, admitted defeat and closed their doors in 1932. They re-opened again briefly in 1950, yet this lasted but a short time, and the

Library exists today as a museum piece, honouring the homage paid to education for all by a Drummond three centuries earlier.

THE GENERAL'S MANGER FOR A CRIB

General Anderson of Elgin gave his money and name to the Elgin Institute, a proud civic building, but perhaps not quite as gracious as the one in which he spent his childhood. For General Anderson, having been deserted by a father he never knew, was brought up in the ruins of Elgin Cathedral by his mother, rose to great heights within the British Army, and, in common with so many successful Scots, marked his success by paving the way for the education and care of others.

In 1851, the custodian of Elgin Cathedral endeavoured to obtain from people then living who had known her, personal facts about the woman who became the mother of the founder of Anderson's Institution. Writing in a swirling and elaborate hand, his must be the most accurate telling of a tale truly of ruin to riches.

Marjory Gilzean was the only child of parents in comfortable circumstances who resided in Drainie and who were greatly respected in the neighbourhood. She was said to be very good-looking and of a sweet and amiable disposition and her worldly prospects were promising. As a young girl she came to know a certain Andrew Anderson, a native of Llanbryde, a soldier whose regiment was quartered in Elgin.

Contrary to the advice and wishes of her immediate family and friends, Marjory married this Anderson in 1745 (the year of the Jacobite Rebellion). Shortly afterwards she left the country with him as soldiers wives did in those days and suffered the 'privations and vissidudes' which commonly fell to the lot of a soldier's wife. The manner in which she had been brought up ill fitted her for enduring the hardships of this wandering life and her husband for whom she had given up so much seems to have treated her badly.

In 1748 three years after her marriage she returned alone to her native land, but with a young child and her mind completely shattered with her misfortunes. Whether or not her parents had died during her absence or still continued to disown her, or were purposely avoided by her, is not know, but having no home and passing through the ruins of Elgin Cathedral, a common footpath led her to the North East corner and a small chamber in a complete state of repair, then (as now) having a roof, chimney, window, walls of solid masonry and the priest's lavatory. An elongated form of basin in which the priests had washed their hands on ceremonial occasions became the crib for her child, and here in this cold cradle amidst desolation, ruin and partial exposure to the elements as they lashed in at the narrow paneless window and along the naked passages, fed and protected by this weak and warmhearted woman, in many ways as helpless as himself, 'baptised in tears and cradled in stone', the future General Anderson was nursed to boyhood.

Fortunately the forlorn condition of this interesting pair excited the sympathies of the benevolent, and so they were seldom allowed to be without plenty of food and winter clothing.

The little boy was put to school as a pauper, cleaning the schoolroom as recompense. He was an industrious scholar as shown by his very successful school records.

Though for a considerable period after her return Marjory lived within this part of the Cathedral, she travelled around the country spinning linen and always had her wheel with her. She also carried a wooden stoup, a container which carried about three pints of whatever her friends would give her.

At one point she seems to have lived in Ballindalloch on the fruits of her spinning and the kindness of neighbours. She was given a black hen, to provide her with a dinner, but then she kept it and it became a companion. She also occupied a wooden shed which stood near the little cross on the south side of South College Street. It was destroyed however, and she returned to her old haunts at the Cathedral.

Here her bed was a bunch of straw and there was no door, but she made one with faggots of broom. Once when she was asked if she was not afraid to live alone in such a dreary place, her reply was

'I'm not afraid of the dead, they are very quiet neighbours, it's the living – if they would let me be.'

About 1788 she went to stay with friends at Lousewort, dying there about 1790.

After her death General Anderson made anxious enquiries on his visit to Elgin in 1811 as to her grave, but the Cathedral custodian could tell him nothing.

Finally he found a stone erected with the inscription:

'Sacred to the memory of
Marjory Gilzean or Anderson who died in 1790
And whose remains lie here interred.'

Later, upon his death was added,

'This stone is erected by the Trustees of her son, General Anderson, The Benevolent Founder of the noble and useful institution which was opened in Elgin in 1832, for the Education of the Young and the Support of Old Age.'

PICTLAND TODAY

The Pictish Kingdom in days of old encompassed the area from Cape Wrath along the rugged coast to John O' Groat's and then swept down to Perthshire and Angus.

The Pictish Kingdom flourished under their kings, and at a famous battle in AD 685, the Pictish King Brude battling against King Ecgfrith of Northumberland, defeated the invading Angles, and, although it was only with hindsight possible to see it was resulting from this event that Scotland stayed Scottish. This battle was fought at Dunnichen, near Forfar and called the Battle of Nechtansmere.

Other invaders tried to break the Scottish hold on their land. There were the plunderers from Norway who eventually established themselves on Shetland and Orkney and the Western Isles, making these lands part of the Norse Kingdom, which effectively threw the Picts together with the Scots, occupying what is today Argyll, Bute and Arran. But even marauding tribes plundering the coasts and searching for slaves did not break the Scots spirit, and the land had remained Scottish, gradually spreading its hold to the borders which we know today. The Picts and Scots became well united through battle and intermarriage, and called their sate, Alba.

Not a great deal more was heard of Pictland for a while, about 1,000 years in fact, when without warning, absolutely no bloodshed, and to the delight of the media, a gentleman named Robbie leapfrogged history and declared himself a Pict.

He renounced his UK citizenship and became a member of Pictland of Alba. His territory is on an acre of land near Tote, south of Staffin on the Isle of Skye. His supporters gradually added 1,000 acres and the Pictish Free State now operates from Robbie's Pictish High Commission.

Things are done quite correctly, according to Robbie, such as leaving the State in a car carrying Diplomatic Corps number plates, which would normally entitle him to freedom from prosecution, but seems to cut little ice with authority on the mainland. One Alness police constable was less than amused to find that he was driving without a tax disc in a car owned by the Pictish Free State. Unfortunately for Robbie this led to one of his 300 prosecutions.

Robbie alias Brian Robertson (1947–), psychology graduate and member of Mensa, founded his state in 1977 and remains staunch and undaunted by the red tape entwining him. He does not hesitate to run the gauntlet of officialdom to sweep out of his State to attend essential celebrations in connection with Pictland.

Every year the members of the Pictish Free State celebrate Dunnichen Day, standing on the hill of that name, which lies three miles to the east of Forfar. From the tip of the hill, the members can survey the ancient battlefield site.

Perhaps the Pictish followers feel safer staying in their haven and proclaiming to the world through a stream of pamphlets.

According to the official literature of the Pictish Free State, the seat of ancient Greek learning was very probably in Strathclyde until a comet destroyed the lost continent of Atlantis, causing the Greeks to leave Scotland for warmer climes.

The River Carron (on the mainland flowing into the sea) has been associated with the mythical Greek ferryman of death, Charon, and the River Styx is identified with the Kyle of Lochalsh (on the mainland ferry crossing to Skye). Further pronouncements declare that indeed the ancient Greek hero Ulysses is likely to have been born in Keppel near Millport and, finally, that Shetlanders are descended from Gad, the lost tribe of Israel.

THE STRANGE TALE OF LADY GRANGE

The curving bay of Ardmore on Skye just to the north of Dunvegan is a far cry from the sophistication of even 18th century Edinburgh, but here lies the body of Lady Rachel Grange, wife of Lord James Erskine, who became a judge and took the title Lord Grange. Her journey from the peak of Edinburgh society to the remote reaches of northern Skye is a tale with all the ingredients of political intrigues, skulduggery and a series of remote hiding places.

Lady Grange, who married her husband in the same year that he became a judge was considered to have made a good match. For his part, Lord Grange had made a strange choice in such a wife. Perhaps it was her beauty which attracted him, although no description or pictures survive to illustrate this, but she was certainly a wilful, strong-minded woman and a staunch Hanovarian. Most startling of all for the wife of an up-and-coming member of the establishment judiciary, she was the daughter of a convicted murderer.

Her father had deserted his wife and children, Rachel among them. The then Lord President, Sir George Lockhart had ordered him to pay alimony. But Rachel's father, a man of explosive, unpredictable temper was outraged at such an order. Rapidly taking the law into his own hands, he promptly shot Lockhart dead when he emerged from attending a church service, a provocative act for which he was convicted and subsequently hanged.

If Lord Grange had chosen to disregard these warning indications of impetuousness, if not insanity, within his wife's family, he also ignored her political leanings. Lord Grange was the brother of Bobbing John, the Earl of Mar, who had led the 1715 rebellion in favour of the Old Pretender, and he himself had Jacobite leanings, although careful to keep such thoughts to himself.

Such a union of opposites might possibly have settled down to domestic bliss, but the battles between them and the emerging signs of Rachel's mental instability turned this into a union that both were to bitterly regret. By 1730 the marriage had acrimoniously disintegrated.

Lady Grange and their children were dispatched to the countryside with £1,000 a year by Lord Grange, but she did not react meekly to the question of banishment. She was a woman who had revelled in the company of the drawing rooms of Edinburgh and who abhorred the idea of being paid alimony like her mother.

Lady Grange fought back with cunning. She knew that her husband was harbouring secret plans to assist the return of the Jacobites, and she had a document to prove this.

She returned to the city, and waving the document underneath his window, shrieked obscenities mingled with revelations as to his political leanings. At first Lord Grange clearly thought that his best policy was to ignore these rantings, and public sympathy was with him, but as the days went on and she appeared again and again, he became alarmed and realised that someone might suspect her stories as being true.

Realising that he was unable to lawfully restrain her, he decided to pursue another route. Nothing in his character suggested that he was anything other than a fair and moderate man, but his actions from then on showed a loss of nerve and a flouting of all he knew to be within the law. For a man in his position it was a measure of the desperation he felt, and a tremendous risk.

When Lord Grange asked Lord Lovat to help 'remove' his wife, he stopped short of requesting her murder. Just after midnight on 22 January 1732, Lovat's trusty followers forced their way into Lady Grange's house in Edinburgh, roughly seized her, resulting in her being bruised, bleeding and having teeth knocked out in the force of the encounter. Lady Grange resisted with all her might, but she was overcome, gagged and galloped through the winter's night, firstly to the house of a MacLeod and then to Wester Polmaise, where she spent thirteen miserable weeks locked up in a room at the top of a tower. Her captors had even taken the precaution of boarding up the window.

Finally, on 30 September, she was moved across Scotland by land and sea to be deposited on the Heisker or Monach Islands, which lie to the west of North Uist. The island was a stronghold of MacDonald of Sleat.

Lady Grange may well have been mentally unstable from time to time, but she knew she had been wronged and was determined to escape. In one attempt, she tried to bribe a local man to row her to the mainland in his boat, but it came to nought as he absconded with the money and worse, her plan was discovered.

So, in June 1734, she was taken to a place of formidable cliffs and isolation from which her captors felt certain she would never leave; St Kilda.

'Oh alas much have I suffere'd often my skin made black and blew, they took me to St Kilda. John MacLeod is called Stewart of the Island he left me in a few days no body lives but the poor native it is a vile, nasty and stinking poor isle.' So ran her account of her latest place of residence.

To Lady Grange, St Kilda must have seemed quite literally like the edge of the world. She was given shelter in a house with a local woman detailed to look after her, but Lady Grange refused both to conform to her captors or to give up hope of rescue. She resolutely refused to communicate more than was necessary with the local St Kildans, who had been instructed to respect this strange foreigner, and who treated her civilly enough. It was simply that she was a woman used to the civilisation of Edinburgh, wrenched away from her children and home, and placed on an island where she could not even communicate with the inhabitants, whose way of life was backward even by the peasant standards of remotest Scotland, and escape from which she gradually became aware was almost impossible.

There were no books, no kindred spirits, nor even the type of food which she could enjoy. The St Kildans lived almost entirely on the flesh of sea birds and their eggs. It was a monotonous existence, made the more so as she had nothing to do, nor would she attempt to adapt and occupy herself.

The steward or 'Stewart' to which she refers came but once a year, and then only if the weather was good. St Kilda was considered a difficult place to visit, and its remoteness gave vent to rumours such as it was a penal colony.

In the meantime in Edinburgh, while Lord Grange showed all the correct signs of a sad widower, explaining away his wife's disappearance as firstly illness, then sudden death, suspicions amongst Lady Grange's family and friends remained alive.

For seven years Lady Grange lived on St Kilda, hanging onto her last remnants of silk clothing, and resolutely refusing to learn Gaelic. Her periods of insanity grew longer, and in her lucid moments she endlessly wrote letters which she tossed into the sea, in the hope of alerting someone to her plight. She slept during the day, and tried to banish the misery of her life with her allowance of whisky.

Finally, a letter she had hidden in a skein of wool leaving St Kilda for the mainland was taken to Inverness. The letter, dated 20 January 1738 finally reached the Solicitor General in 1740, who passed it onto her legal agent, Mr Hope of Rankeillor. Although he was a Jacobite, it was to his credit that he decided to act, and requested a warrant to search St Kilda. Although Lord Grange's legal friends effectively blocked this application for months, eventually the boat was fitted out, filled with armed men and set sail for St Kilda. But the stalling time was to his disadvantage, as when he arrived, Lady Grange had been wafted away.

Mr Hope returned to Edinburgh, satisfied that he had done all he could, and Lady Grange was no longer alive. As soon as all the scares had died down, Lady Grange was removed back to Skye, and once more settled into a cottage at Vaternish, just to the north of Dunvegan, where, two years later, she died.

Even in death, her story was not over. While the MacLeods organised an elaborate funeral which took place at Dunvegan with all due ceremony, and no doubt a large chunk of guilt, the coffin which was lowered into the ground contained not the wasted body of Lady Grange, but a shovelful of earth and a tree trunk. The real funeral, attended by but a handful of MacLeods, took place without much fuss at the tiny, remote, windswept graveyard overlooking Ardmore Bay.

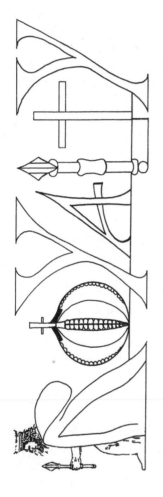

Of Evil
Avalanches
and Lost
Legions,
Kings and
Queens
That Have
Never Been,
and Revealing
Red Lochs.

THE KINGS AND QUEENS THAT NEVER WERE

There were those who claimed that they were the proper heirs to Scottish thrones, and there were Scots who were also asked to take on other Royal titles and risky royal roles abroad. And there again, there were those whose reign came late in the day, and was to all intents and purposes truly over after one fleeting day.

Perhaps some of them might have saved themselves a spot of bother and disappointment by taking a trip to Papa Westray.

According to the 1893 printing of *Folklore of Scottish Lochs and Springs*, St Tredwells Loch, on Papa Westray was in the very regular and reliable habit of turning red whenever anything striking was about to happen to the Royal Family.

FROM ATHOLL TO ALBANIA

In the aftermath of the first world war, when the idea of peace and the unassailable belief in the power of British capabilities were totally accepted, Albania became the strangest country to be mooted as a land ruled by a Scot.

There was no real possibility that the tiny, war torn country should become just another outpost of the Empire. What it should have, declared the Conference of Ambassadors in Paris in 1920, was for them to sort out the borders, protecting them from their neighbours. And what the Albanians wanted, was apparently a British King to come and rule over them, sort them out, and no doubt protect them from the rest of Europe.

The 8th Duke of Atholl was approached. From April to July 1921, he considered the option, along with his wife the politically astute 'Red Duchess'. Although gradually becoming aware that he was also being used as a political pawn, he did consider the matter seriously, even if his wife was less enthusiastic.

If this all sounds an implausible Balkan fairy story, there is written proof of the matter. It is all there, recorded in various memoranda, the diaries of Harold Nicolson and personal papers left behind by the Duke.

The way it came about was this.

The 8th Duke was a second choice to receive an invitation to wear the crown. Aubrey Herbert, an English MP who had become embroiled in the survival of Albania was the first choice. He had been approached, once in 1913 and then just before the Duke of Atholl's name was mooted. He had turned the offer down, both for financial and family reasons, but suggested that the Duke of Atholl seemed a perfect candidate for the job.

Jim Barnes wrote to the Duke, pointing out that of course he should do no more until an offer came (secretly) from Albania, with what sounded less like a romantic introduction to a throne, but more like a job offer with all the conditions spelt out. The Duke should wait until the offer contained details of position, salary, etc, so that he should know exactly what he was letting himself in for.

Jim Barnes concluded that

'Both Herbert and Lord Robert (Cecil) agreed that you are pre-eminently the man for the job because the difficulties you will encounter in Albania are chiefly psychological and there are few people who appear so fitted to understand and fire the imagination of those people as you are. That is half the battle. The rest is statesmanship and there your experience is about as wide as anyone's.'

But the Duke turned down the offer, obviously not feeling that a lifetime spent as a child at Blair Atholl and a career in the army fitted him for elevation into the quagmire of Balkan Royalty. It is quite why he was ever approached that seems oddly unanswered, and what strange underhand negotiations took place which could, in the 20th century, have claimed a Scottish laird for an Albanian throne.

FROM HOME TO ROME

At some point in the 1770s, Prince Charles Edward was eking out his life in Rome, by now married for the second time to Louise, a woman much younger than himself. There was as yet no sign of the much wanted son and heir.

The former Bonnie Prince Charlie was by now far from bonnie. Not only worried by money troubles, he must have been aware that his young wife, bored and perhaps sickened by his drunkenness and obesity was becoming more attached by the day to a responsive poet and playwright, Alfieri. There must also have been lingering background fears about possible assassination attempts.

Into his life came a quite unexpected and unsolicited offer. It came from the land of promise, the New World, the future United States of America. A group of colonists from Boston, clearly disenchanted with the House of Hanover, but enthusiastic about the theory of a Monarchy, suggested that Princes Charles should be crowned their King.

Prince Charles sent off for books and maps about America, such as there were at the time, but the idea was never taken seriously. There is no evidence to suggest that he even considered going there to see for himself.

So with the rejection of this idea, Charles added to his life the epitaph – the King that never was of Scotland, plus the King that never was of the New World.

After the death in 1807 of Henry, the younger brother of the already deceased Bonnie Prince Charlie, the male line of the Stuarts should have come to an end.

The uprising of 1745, and its deterioration into ignominious defeat had effectively scuppered Jacobite hopes, although a loyal few still supported the exiled Prince Charles, who limped into alcoholism and decay.

On Henry's death, it appeared that there were no heirs. But the tale of Prince Charles, the romance of the uprising, the whole aura with which the Stuart Pretenders had been surrounded in popular myth kept hopes high. One of the many writers about this era, Sir Charles Petrie, stated that such was the pull of the Stuart name, any claim to the throne would arouse great passion, whereas if some upstart claimed that he was entitled to be the heir of the Yorkist or Tudor dynasty, then few if any would pay even passing attention.

To this day, the Jacobite cause is seen by many as hovering just above the surface of credibility. Belief in the Stuarts crops up all over Scotland, and across all walks of life, from the crofting highlander buried on the Culloden battle ground, which is almost a shrine to the lost cause, to the great gates at the mansion house of Traquair by Peebles, said to remain closed until a Stuart once more ascends to the throne.

That a Stuart might make a claim could be unlikely, but that the Stuart line did indeed die out, is open to endless speculation.

Like the whole story of the Stuart claim, the story is fanciful and imaginative, running the whole gamut of remote probabilities and with great splashes of romance thrown in.

The basis of the story starts in Italy in 1773, near the Convent of St Rosalie, which is between Parma and Florence. Dr Beaton, a Jacobite exile, was walking in the vicinity when he observed a carriage passing decorated with royal livery, in which there was a woman and a man whom he recognised as Prince Charles.

Later that evening, when he was visiting a local church, a stranger came up to the good doctor, asking him if he would assist at an imminent birth. Dr Beaton was blindfolded, and taken to the house, where he observed two facts. Firstly the lady was safely delivered of a son, and secondly the picture hanging on the wall was a portrait of James III.

Bidden to leave the area immediately, he went to Porto Franconi, and while there noticed an announcement to the effect in the 'Florentine Journal' that the Countess of Albany was now recovered from a recent indisposition. One evening, while again on an evening walk, the doctor saw HMS Albina lying not far from the shore. As he watched, a carriage drove up, accompanied by the horseman whom Dr Beaton recognised as the stranger who had approached him in church, and a lady emerged carrying a baby, stepped into a small boat and this small party was rowed out to the ship lying at anchor.

From this evening in 1773 until 1847, seventy-five years later, the Stuarts disappear from view.

By this year, Queen Victoria was well established on the throne, and a year later she was first to see Balmoral and secure herself within the hearts of the majority of the Scots by making public her love affair with Scotland. In Edinburgh there appeared a book called *Tales of the Century, or Sketches of the Romance of History between the years 1746 and 1846* by two brothers, John Sobieski and Charles Edward Stuart.

The brothers claimed that their father had been the baby borne off on the sea that evening in 1773. He had been brought up by an Admiral John Carter Allen, alongside the Admiral's own son, John. When the Admiral died, he left his estate of £2,300 divided between the two boys, John receiving £2,200 and Thomas, although the elder, only £100.

Thomas, perhaps from financial necessity, joined the Navy, married, lived in France and had two sons. When the boys were sixteen and twelve, their true heritage was revealed to them, and from then on their greatest desire was to return to the land from which their ancestors sprang, although they did have time to fight for Napoleon, perhaps in order to publicly demonstrate their scorn for the Hanover throne.

By 1818 they had arrived in Scotland, and after various wanderings, the marriage of Charles Edward and the arrival of a daughter named Countess Marie, they were befriended by Lord Lovat in 1837, whose offer of a home anywhere on his estate they gladly accepted. The house they chose was on a small island called Eilean Aigas, on the river Beauly, where, according to Flora Fraser, a modern descendant of Lord Lovat, they turned their skills of carpentry to good use to raise the interior of the modest house to a grander effect, more in keeping with their supposed status.

'Busts of Napoleon and of their supposed Stuart forebears jostled with silver pistols once fired by Prince Charlie.'
    'The palace doors they built were flung open ad high backed ceremonial chairs were set behind long trestle tables for royal feasts.'

Four children were born to Charles Edward, and on Sundays this little coterie would proceed to the southern side of the island where a flower-decked barge would take them to the Roman Catholic church of Eskadale.

The brothers were instantly recognisable for their long hair and strange dress, bedecked with tartan.

But by 1846 this idyll was abruptly over and the whole family departed for the Continent. The reason for this sudden move resulted from pique. They had journeyed to Edinburgh in high hopes to attend an assembly at which Queen Victoria was present. Her Majesty, receiving guests in an antechamber was not to honour the anxiously waiting brothers with a call to meet her. Crushed by such a rejection, they departed from Scotland for good.

In later years John Sobieski, having married late in life, haunted the Reading Room of the British Museum attired in outlandish ex-military clothing, by now quite threadbare, with which he sported his spurs. The sight greatly amused the other occupiers of the Museum, but his endless research could do nothing to leapfrog his family from genteel, if entertaining obscurity into the throne of Great Britain.

Of the four children of Charles Edward, one son, named after him, died without issue in 1882. Maria died unmarried, Clemantina became a nun, which left Louisa Sobieski, from whose marriage to the Austro Hungarian Count Von Platt a son was produced. From this son, the ever more remote claim to the Stuart throne then passed.

Perhaps some corner of Scotland is still a resting place of the Stuart Kings. Prince Charles Edward lies in some splendour in a tomb in Rome, but when John Sobieski died in 1872, he was buried in the Eskadale church, under a Celtic cross. Eight years later, he was joined by his brother.

A CORONATION AT KIRK YETHOLM

The Scottish gipsies or travelling folk were not from the same stock as the Romany gipsies, who had travelled across Europe for generations, disregarding state boundaries as far as they could, until at least the Second World War. The gipsies regarded themselves as a race apart, calling themselves Rom, which simply translates as 'man'. They originated in the mountainous regions of Afghanistan or Northern India and migrated westwards.

The Scots travellers were made up of a gaggle of the descendants of those routed at Culloden, wanted men, who had left the glens to fight in the Jacobite cause and never dared to return home for fear of persecution. They came to speak a language called the Cant, which is composed of Gaelic, old Scots and English words, all slightly adapted in their pronunciation.

As the years went by these travellers were swollen by those displaced by the Highland Clearances, and those who were ill-fitted for a static society, who preferred to work in an itinerant fashion. This way of life has continued to a small extent to this day, when travellers still camp out near the raspberry and potato fields, and take on seasonal jobs.

They had their own culture, and for a while their own king and queen. The headquarters of the Royal gipsies was Kirk Yetholm, a small village divided by the Bowmont Water into Kirk Yetholm and Town Yetholm.

Charles Blyth was crowned in Kirk Yetholm in 1847, where there is a small cottage still in existence with a porch and trellised window, which was known as the 'Palace of the Gipsies.'

His daughter, Queen Esther Faa Blythe was buried here in 1883, and it was one of her ancestors, also a former queen, who was reputed to have been the character model for Meg Merrilees in Scott's 'Guy Mannering'.

Her son succeeded her, although he was not crowned until 1898, and he died four years later.

It was his coronation which was recorded on camera, and pictures of the event were numerous. Crowds came to see the coronation, which was just as the organisers had fervently aspired. To all intents and purposes this was a classic media event, choreographed by the unlikely character of the local minister, the Reverend Carrick Miller.

For reasons unknown, there was not going to be another gipsy coronation until the Reverend Miller and a hand-picked committee decided that this would take place. Their motives were entirely straightforward. They wished to catapult the hamlet of Kirk Yetholm into a tourist mecca.

With excellent organisation they certainly attracted huge

crowds, as the contemporary photographs reveal, the centrepiece was the King himself, resplendent in robes hired from a theatrical costumier in Glasgow. It was a popular, but sham coronation.

Having dispensed with the formalities, the King did a roaring trade in autographing pre-taken photos, but being unable to read or write relied on the good auspices of a woman neighbour to help him.

Was it a success promoting Kirk Yetholm as a tourist mecca? Well, who has heard of Kirk Yetholm to this day?

BLACK WATCH

The prowess of the Black Watch Regiment, formerly raised in Perthshire, was and is legendary. They seem to have a knack of landing up in the centre of world events, be they battles or ceremonial occasions. It was no surprise to find them playing on the lawn of the White House days before President Kennedy's assassination. By the special request of Mrs Kennedy, they returned to play for his funeral.

Although they have fought all over the world, they also played a surprising, and prominent part in the American Wars of Independence, where they astonished their enemies by outstanding feats of heroism. Their belief – that a Highlander never retreats – led to fearsome acts of bravery, but also much slaughter of their own ranks. One death, that of Duncan Campbell of Inverawe in 1758, bears a strange witness. Perhaps he may also have been doubly brave, as his death was foretold to him many years earlier.

The accurate telling of this premonition was written down for posterity in the middle of the 19th century by a Dean Stanley and approved as true by his Campbell relatives.

'The ancient castle of Inverawe stands by the banks of the Awe, in the midst of the wild and picturesque scenery of the Western Highlands. Late one evening, before the middle of the last century, as the Laird, Duncan Campbell, sat alone in the old hall, there was a loud knocking at the gate; and opening it, he saw a stranger, with torn clothing and kilt besmeared with blood, who in a breathless voice begged for asylum. He went on to say that he had killed a man in a fray, and that the pursuers were at his heels. Campbell promised to shelter him.

'Swear on your dirk!' said the stranger; and Campbell swore. He then led him to a secret recess in the depths of the castle. Scarcely was he hidden when again there was a loud knocking at the gate, and two armed men again appeared.

'Your cousin Donald has been murdered, and we are looking for the murderer!'

Campbell, remembering his oath, professed to have no knowledge of the fugitive; and the men went on their way. The Laird, in great agitation lay down to rest in a large dark room, where at length he fell asleep. Waking suddenly in bewilderment and terror, he saw the ghost of the murdered Donald standing by his bedside and heard a hollow voice pronounce the words; 'Inverawe! Inverawe! Blood has been shed. Shield not the murderer!'

In the morning, Campbell went to the hiding place of the guilty man and told him he could harbour him no longer.

'You have sworn on your dirk!' he replied; and the Laird of Inverawe, greatly perplexed and troubled, made a compromise between conflicting duties, promised not to betray his guest, led him to the neighbouring mountain (Ben Cruachan) and hid him in a cave.

In the next night, as he lay tossing in feverish slumbers, the same stern voice awoke him, the ghost of his cousin Donald stood again at his bedside and again he heard the appalling words; 'Inverawe! Inverawe! Blood has been shed. Shield not the murderer!'

At break of day he hastened in strange agitation to the cave, but it was empty, the stranger had gone. At night, as he strove in vain to sleep, the vision appeared once more, ghastly pale, but less stern of aspect than before.

'Farewell, Inverawe!' it said; 'Farewell, till we meet at Ticonderoga!'

The strange name dwelt in Campbell's memory, although he had no idea where this place could be.

He had joined the Black Watch, or 42nd Regiment, then

employed in keeping order in the turbulent Highlands. In time, he became a Major; and a year or two after the war broke out, he went to America. Here to his horror, he learnt that it was ordered to the attack of Ticonderoga. His story was well known among his brother officers. They combined among themselves to disarm his fears; and when they reached the fatal spot they told him on the eve of battle,

'This is not Ticonderoga; we are not there yet, this is Fort George.'

But in the morning he came to them with haggard looks.

'I have seen him! You have deceived me! He came to my tent last night! This is Ticonderoga! I shall die today!' and his prediction was fulfilled.'

In fact Duncan Campbell was struck down at the battle, but not mortally. He died nine days later from an infection of his wounds.

This is one of the most famous ghost stories of any Scottish Regiment, and all the circumstantial evidence points to every aspect of the tale being true. Donald was murdered. Ticonderoga, which would have been a foreign enough sounding name to a Scot in the Western Highlands at any time, was unknown to any regiment at the time.

A puzzling twist ends this tale. The grave of Mrs Ann Campbell, wife of Duncan Campbell lies in Gilchrist Lot, Union Cemetery, between the Hudson Falls and Fort Edward. But she died in 1777, over 22 years since the death of her husband. Did she accompany her husband all those years ago? If so, for some reason, she never returned to the family home of Inverawe. One wonders why.

GHOSTLY GIACK

If the Black Watch had a habit of turning up in places which became famous, the story of a Captain McPherson of their Regiment is a further ghostly addition.

Captain McPherson and four others were stationed at the Old Lodge of Giack, an area considered isolated even in those days, and with an ominous and overwhelming feeling of malevolence. Many writers have told of tales of evil supernatural there – long before the events related here – but it is in more tangible disasters that the true nature of the area reveals itself.

Giack Lodge sits in the centre of a flat-bottomed glen, nestling between two ridges of mountains, both of which rise to almost 3,000 feet. On New Years Eve, 1799, an avalanche swept down one side of the mountain, killing all five men. A few days later, goes the tale, the remainder of the Lodge was mysteriously and totally destroyed.

This avalanche is meant to strike around every hundred years, and sure enough, in 1911 yet another powerful fall missed the replaced Giack Lodge by a matter of yards. What will the 21st century bring?

FLOWER POWER

In the pre-commuter days when paybooks were carried around by soldiers, those belonging to the Gordon Highlanders, based in Aberdeen, were unique in that they contained a sprig of white heather.

During Wars, when the regiment would move around a great deal, and no one was any too sure where they would be off to next, this precious paybook was the enveloping cover for the heather, given by wives, sweethearts or mothers as a symbol of good luck.

MOSCOW

The sign is clearly spelt out, just three miles off the A71 on the route from the M74 to Prestwick Airport.

There is the village of Moscow sitting on the River Volga, with two neighbouring farms rejoicing in the names of Higher and Lower Rushaw.

It has been conjectured that these places were christened during the Napoleonic Wars, when it became fashionable to use names made famous by the activities of the French emperor. Local rumour has suggested that there may have been a prisoner of war camp here in the Crimean Wars. But the truth is stranger than this, for the names well pre-date this era. One fact is certain. Moscow, Ayrshire, has no connection with its larger namesake, and the River Volga no common water with its much more powerful twin.

No one knows why these places are so named, but the most likely derivation is that it was a corruption of the Norman 'Mosshall' to 'Moss haw', and these names stuck for many a long century. But when in the early part of the 19th century the news reached this part of the country, perhaps some wag found it an easy joke.

EDINBURGH CASTLE

The year is 1137 and the scene is the Town Planning Department of the city of Edinburgh. The Director of Town Planning is making a phone call.

'Hello, is that King Malcolm of Scotland? Good morning. Director of Town Planning here. Sorry to bother you, but I've got your application here for outline planning permission and there are just one or two points I'd like to get cleared up. Now have I got this right? You're proposing to build some kind of castle, bang in the middle of Edinburgh, on top of that lump of rock overlooking Princes Street Gardens and Waverley Station. Now is that right? Because if it is, Your Majesty, you're away with the fairies. All these years of royal inbreeding must be catching up with you. No, no. No disrespect, Your Majesty, but I mean to say, a great monstrosity of a castle, sticking up like a sore thumb, directly opposite two of Scotland's finest natural treasures – British Home Stores and Marks and Spencer. It'll ruin the whole character of the city.

'And I'll tell you this, you're going to have some fearful technical difficulties. I mean, that's solid volcanic rock there. How are you going to get a sewage pipe through it? Well, but as I understand it, Your Majesty, you're going to have a garrison of 500 troops there. What arrangements are you going to make for sewage? A chain of buckets? All the way down to the Forth? That's a lot of buckets. I mean to say, we are living in the twelfth century after all. The Environmental Health people just won't wear it, Your Majesty. The Environmental Health, Your Majesty. Used to be called the Sanitary Inspector, before the 1066 re-organisation.

'Now, what else was I going to ask you? Sorry, I'm a bit woozy this morning, but I was at the Watsonian dinner last night. I saw your son there – the heir to the throne. But he's not a Watsonian. No you couldn't get him into Watsons. Where did you get him in? Stewarts-Melville? Dear God. But he got kicked out of there, and he's in Borstal now. Oh well, it's not as bad as Stewarts-Melville.

'There's a word here on the plan that I can't quite read. It looks like 'gun', but it can't be 'gun'. What's that? It is 'gun'. Every day at 1 o'clock, you propose to fire off a gun from the castle. What on earth for? To let people know what time it is? But there's a perfectly good clock on the top of the North British Hotel (now the Balmoral). And I'll tell you this. If you're going to be firing off artillery from the domestic premises, you've really got to watch it. Have you served notice on adjoining properties? 'Cos you've got a guy down the road from you there on the Royal Mile – John Knox – a right bloody killjoy, I can tell you. I don't know what he does for a living, but there's not an ounce of Christian charity about him.

'Now, have you got an architect for this harebrained scheme. I only ask, because there's no name at the bottom of the plan. And in my experience that means you've got someone from the City Architect's department to do a homer. You have? Who did you get exactly? The City Architect himself? Well, with him as your architect, you'll need a damn good contractor. Who have you got? Barratt's. And the best of British luck to you. Oh, no I quite agree, their publicity is very good. Of course they've got a helicopter, specially invented for them by Leonardo da Vinci. And they've opened a new European division. They've just built a tower, at Pisa. And from all accounts they haven't got it quite right.

'Well, well, to get back to your application, it is very unusual. I mean, the kind of thing I usually deal with is – well, like the application I had yesterday, for a double lock up in Corstorphine. Even that was tricky. I'd a helluva job finding a good reason to throw it out. It was quite attractive – pebble dash finish with an up and over door. Something like that would look quite nice on top of that rock. Or what about a nice wee factory, with plenty of concrete and galvanised steel? Or could you not put up an office block like everything else? There's never any planning difficulty with that kind of thing...'

(With thanks to *Scotland the What?*)

THE LOST ROMAN LEGION OF THE 9TH

It was shortly into this millennium around the year AD 117 that the Roman legion of the 9th, fearsome warriors all, marched north in yet another attempt to subdue the woad-dyed tribes who repeatedly caused the Romans more trouble than all the English between them.

The 9th Legion would carry their golden eagle on its staff at the head of the marching men.

At the time, the Legion were supposedly stationed at Eburacum, close to where York now stands, and after they marched north, into the lands where Perthshire now spreads, they vanished. It is a mysterious and romantic tale in the best traditions, and indeed that crack storyteller for children, Rosemary Sutcliffe, took the bare bones of the tale and turned it into a gripping story.

Her story was based on one young soldier, whose father had been one of the commanders of the 9th, and who sought to find out what had happened to the Legion. North he marched, disguised as a travelling Egyptian occultist, and finally found the remains of the eagle in a place of heathen worship, just escaping with his life.

Rosemary Sutcliffe based her story on two facts. Firstly that the 9th Legion had been stationed at Eburacum. Secondly that during the excavations at Silchester nearly 1,800 years later, a wingless eagle was found, the cast of which can be seen in Reading Museum. Both facts are true. Her story tells of the Legion simply disintegrating. Morale must have suffered, deserters became rife, it was an ignominious end, as the weakened and scattered remnants of the Legion were eroded by marauding locals, and disgraced, the remainder of the Legion were murdered or integrated into the glens. So her story poses many unanswered questions. Are some of us reading this today descended from this possibly disgraced Roman rabble? Italian blood integrated into the glens of Scotland long before the advent of the ice cream parlour or spaghetti house?

Who knows?

Professor Colin Martin, actually. A lecturer in history at St Andrews University, he dispels this myth in a trice.

The Legion of the 9th certainly did march off from Eburacum. But in a different direction. They were rather mysteriously and abruptly summoned home and then dispatched to what is now Palestine, where they did in fact end their career in disgrace, and were disbanded.

From the misty northern climes of Scotland to the heat of the Middle East. How could such a story have changed its location, if indeed it did? We can but conjecture.

Heathery Marriage Knot, Protective Rowans, Curing Foxgloves, Saintly St Johns Wort and Loyal Lupins. Gaelic Times to Sew and Times to Reap and Beltane Bannocks and 'Brocken' Milk.

MYSTICAL PLANT PURPOSES

Plants were valued for medicine and food. But just as vital were the mystical powers they were thought to convey. There seems to be little obvious reasoning in some of the traditions, but their convenience, even being used recently, cannot be underestimated.

WHITE HEATHER PROPOSAL

The giving of a sprig of white heather as a token of luck is still much practised. Brides carry a sprig of the heather in flower, and once upon a time the gift of a sprig was deemed to be a wedding proposal.

Andrew McGregor McKay, the gamekeeper of the Kildrummy Estate on Donside brought a bunch of white heather off the hill and presented it to the cook at the big house. Apparently he was unaware of the significance of this. But the cook took him very seriously, and would not release him, so the story goes. They married and lived together happily ever afterwards.

Other plants conveyed luck, guaranteed immunity from evil deeds, and spun their own personal tale.

CAMPANULA

All over the country, the pretty bluebell (Campanula rotundifolia) was called the witchbell flower, a protection from wickedness.

HONEYSUCKLE

An old custom on the west coast of Scotland was that on the night of 2 May, people would hang a branch of honeysuckle in their byres, to keep the cattle from being bewitched.

ASH

In the Borders, boys prefer a herding stick made of Ash, to that of another type of wood, because it is sure not to strike any vital part of the animal at which it may be thrown.

GORSE

'When the gorse is oot o' bloom,
Kissin's oot o' fashion'

So goes the old saying, wisely put, as gorse is a year round flowering plant, but to pick a sprig of it was deemed in Fife to be very unlucky, either to give or be given it blooms.

ROWAN TREES

The Reverend W. Grigor, a great recorder of superstitions, wrote in 1888 that 'to keep the witches at a distance, there were various methods and all of approved value. On bonfire night (Festival of Beltane) small pieces of Rowan Tree and Woodbine were placed over the byre doors inside the house. Sometimes it was a single rod of Rowan, covered with notches'. There is a well known rhyme:

The Rawn tree in the widd-bin
Haud the witches on cum in.

Or Rawn tree in red thread
Pits the witches t' their speed.

Rawn tree in red thread
Gars the witches tyne their speed.

The same rector also noted that

'Our Scottish neighbours hold, according to Dr Jamieson that "the most approved charm against cantrips (magic) and spells was a branch of the rowan tree planted and placed over the byre (cowhouse or dwelling). This sacred tree cannot be removed by unholy fingers"'.

For

> Roan tree and red thread
> Haud the witches a in dread.

Among the Highlanders, red thread is tied round the tales of the cattle before they are sent out to pasture in spring, and the women keep off witches from their persons by tying red silk round their own fingers.

Plants and folklore intermingled in medicine. Some of the practices were founded in lost mysticism... others perhaps less so.

THE FOXGLOVE ROOTS

Cure made by an old lady from the Braes of Lochaber, with a recipe which she had learnt from her mother. For a great pain from internal growth or swelling, a pulp was made from squashed foxglove roots, then applied with a flannel, after the pulp had been heated, as a poultice to the swelling. The man received immediate relief and continued to do so until the cure was completed.

THE CURE OF ST JOHN

St John's Wort (hypericum perforatum) which grew widespread all over Scotland was used extensively for the dressing of wounds. Unknown to those ancient practitioners of self treatment, this plant contains allantoin, which helps to proliferate tissue.

For some reason, the flower has also become associated with the devil and on the saints' day, St John the Baptist, 24 June, it was hung up and burnt for the destruction of evil and as a safeguard against witchcraft.

Perhaps it is that 24 June is so close to midsummer's day, and the brilliant yellow of the flower is akin to that of the sun; the association of the flower with pagan rites and Christianity are blurred.

Such was the importance attached to St John's Wort, that St

Columba was reputed to have carried seeds of the plant from Ireland, under his armpit to Iona, no doubt in case he was unable to locate this vital flower growing on the island. St John's Wort was closely tied in with strong religious belief in its power. The reddish coloured sap was described as the blood of St John.

SHOCK TREATMENT

Many cures were tried to treat people with mental illness on the more remote parts of Scotland. Marching the patient round anything holy in midsummer was much practised, leaving the poor victim near an altar overnight, or dousing with water which had religious qualities.

On Skye, and perhaps on other outlying parts of the country, a forerunner of electrical shock was carefully noted by Martin Martin when he wrote in 1716 in *The Description of the Western Islands*.

'The patient being laid on the anvil with his Face uppermost, the smith takes a big Hammer in both his Hands, and making the Face all Grimace, he approaches his Patient; and then drawing his hammer from the Ground, as if he design'd to hit him with his full strength on the Forehead he ends in a Feint, else he would be sure to cure the patient of all diseases: but the Smith being accustomed to the Performance, has a dexterity of managing his Hammer with Discretion; tho at the same time he must do it so as to strike terror in the patient and this they say has always the design't effect.'

MACDONALD'S DISEASE

Tinneas nan Domhnullach, also called Glacach was the name given to a disease of the chest, supposedly curable by the reciting of a verse over the patient, and the touch of the right hand of a MacDonald.

In 1772, note was taken of 'An affection of the lungs, believed to be cured miraculously by particular members of the family of

MacDonald of the Isles,' a statement confirmed a few years later in the Statistical Account of 1795;

> 'It is called the Macdonald's disease because there are partic-
> ular tribes of MacDonalds who are believed to cure it with the
> charm of their touch and the use of a certain set of words.
> There must be not fee given of any kind.'

THE MARCH OF THE LARCH

The modern forests of Scotland are quite different from the old pines, oaks and birch which swathed huge areas until the felling of timber for the great smelting industries.

Jigsaws of evergreens and larches now blanket acres of hillside. The sight of fresh green leaves of springtime larches are but a modern addition to the greenery of Scotland, introduced by the 2nd Duke of Atholl, who in 1738 planted five European larch seedlings on a piece of his own ground, the lawn between the Cathedral at Dunkeld and the River Tay.

Many years later, the progeny of these seedlings spread throughout the estate. From these five trees which became known as the parent larches for which Dunkeld was to become famous, one still survives, and bred a valuable income for future Dukes of Atholl, who were not slow to capitalise on their value. This 250 year old tree stands just over 100 feet (30 metres) tall with a wide crown and a well developed 'hangman's branch', which leaves the trunk horizontally and at 8 to 10 feet (2.4 to 3 metres) out, turns abruptly to the perpendicular.

Perchance the reason for planting in such a spot was simply to protect them from nibbling deer, who would have shied away from such a position close to habitation, and also bounded on one side by the fast flowing Tay. Or perhaps the 2nd Duke planted these delicate young seedlings with a less altruistic approach. It would be pleasant to surmise that one of the reasons they were so close to the Cathedral was to bless their life. After all, the Cathedral had been founded in 315 AD by missionaries of Columba, and had become the centre of the Scottish Church when Iona was no longer safe from the marauding Vikings.

Not only does one of the original larches survive, soaring up by the Cathedral, but also at Birnam, downriver from Dunkeld, grows the largest sycamore tree in Britain, leaning in a neighbourly fashion towards the famous Birnam oak. This is the remnant of the sweeping oak forests which covered the area in the 11th century and which have been immortalised in Shakespeare's *Macbeth*… 'Fear not till Birnam woods come to Dunsinane'.

Perhaps mindful of the extensive use of oak in the ships of the British navy, the next Duke of Atholl looked out in the early 1800s over his inherited forests and determined to use his larches for boats. (Larch is still used to this day for making salmon fishing cobbles used on the Tay.)

He hastened to local Perth shipbuilder, Mr James Brown, a gentleman who had distinguished himself by supervising the raising of the Comet steam vessel after she had been long sunk in the Clyde. The Duke prevailed upon Mr Brown to construct a ship entirely of larch from his estate, to prove a point. And upon completion, the Duke himself launched the boat in considerable style. Contemporary accounts describe the scene where an assembly of nobility and gentry sheltered under a large marquee and were given an 'elegant entertainment'.

The vessel acquitted itself in style, and spent many years sailing the seas until she sank in the Black Sea. Two years later she was salvaged and the timbers were found to be as fresh as the day she was built.

Armed with such encouraging news, the Duke prevailed upon the Naval Sea Lords to try out larch for their ships. Accordingly, the 'Athole' a frigate of 36 guns was built of larch and sent out to foreign service. Years later, she was taken into dry dock, and carefully inspected alongside another frigate of oak, which had been built at the same time. No doubt the Duke was only too pleased to receive confirmation of his beliefs as 'it was found that the timbers of the Athole were quite sound, while those of the other were completely rotten.'

One would have expected no less from trees whose forebears grew up within the shadow of Dunkeld Cathedral.

The pointed tops of the fir trees which then proceeded to cover parts of Scotland gave rise to new expressions.

In Glen Clova, when there was a drab, windless, wet day, the wisps of damp cloud which hung above the trees were known locally as 'tinkie reeks' as they looked just like the thin wisps of smoke which used to be seen, rising up from a gipsy encampment.

FLOWERY BANKS
OF THE FLOWING DEE

Mists of blues and pinks, creeping down the Aberdeenshire Dee year by year, the common Lupin was neither common nor planted for a commoner.

A sack of seeds were brought to Queen Victoria as a present, so the story goes, and cast into the Dee by a gardener, to make an enchanted fringe of flowers for a much loved Royal river.

GAELIC DAYS
OF THE WEEK

What's in a name? In Gaelic-speaking parts of the country each and every day had a meaning, and a built-in set of ground rules, along with the sure retribution if these were infringed...

Di-Domhnaich – Sunday

The day of the Lord, plants pulled on a Sunday are without harm or good.

Di-Luain – Monday, or Moonday

It was unlucky to start ploughing on Monday or to start any other work. But it was considered a good day for 'flitting' just as Saturday was the reverse. It was known as the key of the week, (iuchair na seachdair).

Di-Mairt – Tuesday

A good day to begin ploughing but it was unlucky if the harness broke and the ploughing was stopped.

Di-Ciadair – Wednesday

In some parts of the Highlands sowing the seed was only done on Wednesday or Thursday.

Di-Rdaoin – Thursday

The lucky day for the birth of a calf or lamb, for beginning to weave or for cutting the hair or the beard. It is unlucky for Beltane to fall on a Thursday and Samkaim to fall on a Wednesday.

In Shetland weddings generally took place on a Thursday since Thor was meant to have a special blessing for the bride and groom.

Di-Haoine – Friday

On Friday and Sunday it was unlucky to visit the sick. Many believed that this caused a death in the house. No iron might enter the ground and therefore no ploughing or grave digging took place on a Friday. It was unlucky to cut hair or nails, to sharpen knives, to begin any work, to count animals or go near the fire. Work begun on Friday was said to be too hurriedly done. A person born on Friday was said to be always in a hurry...

a curse was:

'Ruith na h'aoine ort (The hurry or running of Friday be on you).

Di-Sathuirne – Saturday

It was unlucky to prepare for weaving on Saturday, and a common curse was:

'The warp prepared on Saturday will have the delay of the seven Saturdays upon it.'

No spinning might be done after sunset, and all work should stop at 9pm. The New moon on Saturday foretold stormy weather saying,

'The Saturday light goes seven times mad before it goes out.'

THE BELTANE BANNOCKS AND FIRES

Of all the great Pagan Festivals, Hallowe'en is the one still celebrated today, but Beltane which took place at the beginning of May, was rich in legend and ceremony.

The name, Beltane means not only the day, but perhaps sometimes also the season, which is equivalent to Whitsuntide.

Today there are strong relics of this Druidical festival. About eight miles north of Perth is the area of Tullybelton, formerly called Tullibeltane.

'In the neighbourhood,' says Dr Jamieson, author of an early Scottish dictionary, 'is a Druidical temple of eight upright stones, where it is supposed the fire was kindled. At some distance from this is another temple of the same kind, but smaller, and near is a well, still held in great veneration. On Beltane morning superstitious people go to this well and drink of it; then they make a procession round it nine times. After this they in like manner go round the temple.'

In old Gaelic literature there are many references to Bealltuinn, or Beltane.

Nine was the sacred number in Druidical times, hence the number of turns here and the number of knobs on the Beltane cakes. Celtic veneration for the sun appears too, in the way the pilgrims to the well would go around it. All would follow the course of the sun, 'deas iuil,' the lucky way, while the opposite is 'tuath-ivil' or the way that would make their pilgrimage bring misfortune to them.

The yellow Day of Beltane, the great festival, also seemed to welcome the commencement of summer. It was a day to celebrate fire and sun worship, perhaps to welcome the beginning of summer. The date varied, but it was always very close to the beginning of May.

The events which took place were recorded by Cormac, who describes how the Druids made two fires by rubbing sticks together, or rubbing wood hard against iron, chanted an incantation while doing this. After the flame was kindled, fires in the surrounding houses were extinguished and relit from this 'new' flame. Cormac also describes how the people would bring their cattle together to the knoll and drive them between two fires in order to preserve the beasts against disease.

As late as 1790, this custom of celebrating Beltane was still being practised. The Statistical Account from the Parish of Callander describes:

'Upon the first of May which is called Beltane all the boys in a township or hamlet meet on the moors. They cut a table in the green sod of a round shape by casting a trench in the ground of such a circumference as to hold the whole company. They kindle the fire and dress a repast of eggs and milk in the consistency of a custard. They knead a cake of oatmeal which is toasted in the embers against a stone.

'After the custard is eaten they divide the cake into as many portions as they are persons in the company. They daub one of these portions all over with charcoal until it be perfectly black. They put all the bits of the cake into a bonnet. Whoever draws out the black bit is the devoted person who is to be sacrificed to the God, whose favour they implore in rendering the year productive of sustenance for man and beast. There is little doubt of these human sacrifices having been once offered in this country although they now only compel the devoted person to leap three times through the flames, with which the ceremonies of the festivals are closed. The Beltane ceremonies have faded out amongst us much more quickly than those of Halloween...'

Dr Sinton in his book *By Loch and River* (he was born in Aberader in the year 1857) writes that

'Every year when Beltane grew near, the villagers of Kingussie were occupied with two weighty matters, which at that time always claimed their attention; – the preparation of Beltane Bannocks and casting peats. May Day festival has latterly been degenerated, like that of St Bride to merely childrens' pastimes. Thick rounds of cakes and oatmeal, covered on both sides with a firm layer of custard were made, and fired carefully with a view to rolling well. Then when Beltane morning came, family parties, carrying their bannocks and hard boiled eggs, might be seen gaily winding their steps to smooth green slopes facing the sun, where with shouts of laughter intermingled with the music of wood and roll and cuckoo's occasional cry, I have known the fun go on until noon – the bannocks and eggs being rolled again and again from the top to the foot of some long declivity.'

HALLOWE'EN

Hallowe'en is now but a celebration for children, to dress up as witches or wicked ghosts and chant verses in return for small rewards. Years ago, the association of Hallowe'en as a time when the future or past would be revealed was widespread.

The custom was immortalised in Burns' poem *Hallowe'en*.

One rendering of the tradition was well defined. If a girl wanted to see the wraith, ghost or apparition of her future husband, she was to go to a place where the lands of three lairds met, by a burn, and dip her left sark sleeve in the burn, turn it inside out, go home and hang it up before the fire and hide away, either in a bed or in the corner. She was then to watch to see who came.

In 1970 Tom Moncrieffe of Virkie, Shetland, told the following version of this tale to Alan Bruford.

'I remember hearing that a girl had nearly brought misfortune, according to the story, on her future husband. She had dipped the sark sleeve in the burn and hung it up, turned it inside out, an then she hid away in the corner, and the apparition came in, a young man in sailor's clothing, and he turned the sleeve around and hung it back. And she was so curious to see him again that she went and turned the sleeve outside in and hung it back, and he came back and turned it again. And not content even with the second appearance, she invoked a third appearance and that time he left a sheath knife.

And years later, when she was married to him – she'd hidden the knife in an old chest – he came across it and recognised it. He asked her how on earth she got that knife and she told him about this ploy which they had played at Hallowe'en.

And he said, well, if I had known that, you should never have been married to me, for I was at sea that night and I was three times overboard, and, he said the last time, I lost my knife and I nearly lost my life.'

HARVEST CUSTOM

'After the Harvest had been gathered, it was the custom of a farmer at Nethybridge to entertain the farm workers and neighbours to a Harvest Home.

At the commencement of the supper, a large bowl of whipped milk, or 'Brocken Milk' as it was called, was placed on the table, before it was served (together with a large home-baked pancake) to each guest, one and all had to beat up the contents with a froth stick. This was a round piece of wood with a hole in the centre which held the stick of handle. The wooden disc was grooved, and round this was wound a wisp of cow hair, taken from the animal's tail. Any guest who did not take part in this procedure would have bad 'buidseachd' and the cream would not come.'

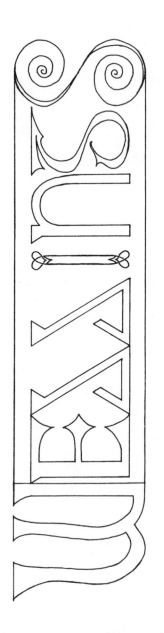

Wedding
Knolls, Kissing
Dances, Bridal
Sheep,
Stealing Reels,
Rigadoon-a-
Daisy and
Romantic
Heart of
Stones.

SCOTTISH WEDDINGS

The importance attached to celebrating weddings in Scotland is an eye-opener to those with a dour image of the Scots race. Of all the great events in life, weddings still to this day require a master-minding of organisation and a generous purse – as the event is rarely less than a twelve hour marathon.

Three day celebrations among the farming folk of the north east are of post-war memory. Even today, the very least in which a couple are expected to participate is a full scale marriage ceremony either in church or registry office followed by a smallish 'breakfast' for the invited close relatives, then a lull before the wedding dance proper, which takes place in the evening and to which all not invited to the 'breakfast' then join in.

In the exuberance with which the Scots celebrate their weddings, they dispel any lingering myths of a gloomy race. The jollity, dancing, feasting and dressing up are far more akin to the great wedding celebrations of the Mediterranean countries.

That a wedding was a good chance to let one's hair down was a well accepted fact. Amidst the small communities, there are few tales of elopement or of a couple trying to escape this ebullient rite of passage. There was also a general acceptance that in the heat of the moment, those who wished to overindulge would inevitably do so. In some areas of the Moray coast, typically in Buckie, the lucky couple were required to make a deposit against these high spirits spilling over into unseemly behaviour and resulting in a good old fisticuffs. They would have to place half a guinea with the town fathers. If all went well, the money would be returned. If things deteriorated into a brawl, then the money was given to the poor.

That a wedding was the high spot in any village calendar was accepted. For from disapproving of the flamboyance of behaviour or the extravagance of food and clothes in a poor area, many minis-ters were careful to scrutinise every nuance of the day, and minutely record the event. Very fortunately, many Kirk ministers were fascinated by the celebrations organised by their flock, and chose to disregard the superstitions and pagan overtones which accompanied the events.

Mainly from these writings, the minutiae of the Scottish wedding in all its forms has passed down to future generations. Little did they know how few of the customs would survive even a century. The Reverend J. Moir Porteus, writing in *God's Treasure House in Scotland*, published in 1876 describes weddings at his local village, Wanlockhead in Dumfries-shire (the highest village in Scotland).

'A marriage at the village is generally an occasion of rejoicing and is the chief topic discussed for a length of time. When a member of the band is married, the whole population turns out to witness the procession; sounds of marital music are heard in the distance and then more plainly reverberating amongst the hills, until, preceded by the brass band of the village, the bridegroom and his party of friends are conducted to the cottage of the bride's friends. By her side the bridegroom takes his place; and in reply to the questioning of the village pastor, and in the presence of as many friends as can be crowded into the little kitchen, he vows to be unto her a faithful and loving husband till death shall part them.

The necessary document being duly signed and attested, congratulations over, refreshments partaken of, these and in the other cottages filled with friends, pence collection and handed to the minister, the best man then comes forward and offers his arm to the bride to head the procession which two and two goes forward, the bridegroom being bought on at the end by the father, along with the minister. The band in their smart apparel, having formed at the door, precedes, playing their liveliest tunes. The bride, of course is the centre of attraction, especially to the wives and daughters, who plaids over heads, press forward to get a close inspection and such notes of admiration are heard as "Eh! but she is braw and bonny."

Arriving at the new dwelling which is furnished with drawers, cupboards presents and necessaries, the new wife, who is saluted with a shower of oatcakes, is let to the fireside to 'poke the ribs' with the tongs in proof that she has taken possession: and then again, at the head of the procession the company are at length seated at tables laden with good things in a room or rooms (no proper hall as yet possessed).

These having been partaken of, the company, crossing their arms and joining hands sing:

> "Weel may we a' be,
> Ill may we never see,
> God bless the Queen
> And this companie".

Three times this is repeated, 'to flie the rattens' with rounds of applause, and the ceremonies being concluded in truly orthodox fashion, the minister retires and the ladies prepare for the evenings enjoyment.'

ROMANTIC HEART OF STONES

Travelling folk, nicknamed tinkers because of the tinking sounds made by their cans and buckets, gathered around the Blairgowrie area in Perthshire.

In the summer months, they worked on the raspberry fields picking, always returning to the same farm for work each summer. In the autumn there were the tatties to lift, and then over the winter, for a few, there was the cutting out of old raspberry canes and tying in the new ones, and other odd seasonal farm jobs.

There were but a few families, and they tended to marry into one another. They were of staunch character, and once married usually remained resolutely faithful. Children were much loved, and accepted as being the responsibility not only of the immediate parents, but of all the group.

Travelling folk were frequently married by one of their own folk. Embedded into the road near Strachur, Argyll, is a stone 'heart' inlaid using large pebbles. No one is sure why this spot was chosen, but it has been used for at least two centuries.

At this remote and beautiful place may gipsy weddings were solemnised. Today, marriages there are unknown, but it has been adopted as an impromptu proposal spot for modern day romantics.

But at Little Dunkeld where many of the travellers assembled during the summer season, proper church weddings were frequent. It was a natural place for this to occur. All the families met together for several weeks. During the Second World War, more travellers than ever suddenly appeared to be wed, even if they had lived together as man and wife for years. One, who had been living with his wife for 24 years and had seven children by her thought that he might be called up for military service, and thus rushed to be wed. It was much easier to for wives to obtain allowances if they had marriage documentation.

Redolent of a staid and conformist reason, it was a far cry from the wedding hearts at Strachur.

On the Isle of Ulva, which lies just to the west of Mull, an old custom declared that when a tenant married, he would pay a due to the laird, which was generally one of his sheep. This might have seemed a reversal of traditional gifting for weddings, surely the lucky couple should be recipients of presents not the other way around? However, as the modern day guide book for Ulva points out, this was not only the way things were done, but exceptionally enlightened behaviour for the times (pre this century) as elsewhere the laird would demand that the bride spent her wedding night with him.

Edward Burt, a travelling writer wrote a letter in 1726 describing Penny Weddings.

'They have a penny wedding, that is when a servant maid has served faithfully and gained the good will of her master and mistress, they invite their relations and friends and there is a dinner or supper on the day the servant is married, and music and dancing to follow to complete the evening.

'The bride must go about the room and kiss every man in the company, and in the end everybody puts money into a dish, according to their inclination and ability. By this means a family in good circumstances and respected by those they invite, have procured for the new couple where withal to begin the world pretty comfortably for people of their low condition. But I should have told you that the whole expense of the fee and fiddlers is paid out of the contribution. This and the former are likewise custom all over the Lowlands of Scotland.'

Another custom which took place mainly in the Borders, but was heard of in other parts of the land too was the 'basiller', the title given to money which was scattered at a wedding for children to scramble for.

In other parts of Scotland, another custom for meeting the cost of the celebration was an 'inpit wedding', where the guests contributed by the women bringing the cakes and the men the whisky.

In Inverness,

'The bride must have nothing to do with the making of the wedding dress and must not even try it on in its entirety before the wedding day, as that would mean dire misfortune. In her right stocking, she should ship a small silver coin and for it the bridesmaids strive when they disrobe her at night. If she has previously given encouragement to other sweet-hearts, she had better leave a coin in her left stocking until she has been kirked. To put on the left shoe before the right on this morning is also likely to bring unhappiness; and when fully dressed in:

'Something old and something new
Something borrowed, something blue.'

She must not look in the mirror even to see if everything

is on all right, neither must she turn after she has once set out.'

In the East Neuk of Fife there were equally steadfast customs.

It is not surprising that fishing marriages were encompassed by more traditions than many others, as all round the east coast and the islands, where a precarious livelihood was wrenched out of the sea, life was filled with such potential hazards that every expression and rite of passage in life was encumbered by paying verbal insurances to the fates. Most weddings were solemnised by the minister, either in the manse, the town hall or even at home. Following the service, the wedding supper was eaten by all the guests. Those unable to come were sent out plates of food, and the 'bride's plate', which was the first dish to leave the door, was for an especially honoured friend of the family, someone who was not a relation, but a much cherished family friend.

In places as far apart as Orkney and Auchmithie, on the Aberdeenshire coast the bride and groom would lead almost the entire wedding party on a long walk round the village or hamlet. This 'long walk' was a noted tradition in Orkney while 'At Kilbarchan,' wrote J. Paterson in his *Sempil Poem*, 'the bride and her maidens would walk three times round the Church before the marriage was celebrated, led on by a piper who played some peculiar tune, which got he named "Maiden trace".'

In Unst, on the Shetland Islands, weddings traditionally took place in the winter months when there was less work to be done and people could throw themselves wholeheartedly into the celebrations. Everyone in the vicinity was invited, and the celebrations fell roughly into a three day event.

The day before the wedding, relatives and guests would assemble, and using planks of wood from any source (driftwood was the most common) would make a temporary floor for an empty barn.

The wedding day started off with a lengthy wedding breakfast, followed by the company walking to the church, with everyone dressed in their best. Men wore white gloves and mufflers, the women wore white gloves and scarves and everyone sported flowers. The bride's white veil was knitted in white openwork wool.

Last in the procession to church came the groom's youngest brother and the bride's youngest sister, trailing a straw brush behind her, to symbolically sweep clean behind them.

Two 'gunners' ran along the line of the wedding party triggering off their firearms periodically, and each time a shot rang out, the crowd cheered. Armed as they were with blunderbuss which they filled with powder and paper wadding, the gunners entered into the festive spirit of the day by banging away whenever they felt like it. As a result the wedding guests would run the gauntlet of flaming pieces of paper floating down on the wind.

The return route from the church was the 'long walk' when the bride and groom led the guests on a circuitous route round the village until they arrived back at the house, turned round and welcomed the guests into the house.

After the dinner had been eaten, the guests went out for a walk, while the room or barn was cleared, and dancing followed, with at least two fiddlers, one at each end of the barn.

Each man brought a stone of sweets to the wedding and when the dancing began, he went round the house and gave a handful of sweets to each girl in the place and gave the bag to his own partner for her to carry her own sweets in. Additionally, everyone received a bag of sweets to take home.

Bride and groom visited any sick friend during the night. The guests had supper and danced till dawn, liberally supplied with refreshments. At dawn, they had breakfast, went home, returned for lunch and a repeat of the previous evening's performance. At the second dawn, guests thanked their hosts and were speeded on their way by more refreshments.

Thus ended the wedding!

WEDDING DANCES

Surprisingly little remains recorded about traditional wedding dances, certainly they have nearly or totally died out, but in *Traditional dancing in Scotland* by Flett, many hints are given about the important role a special dance played in the whole wedding celebration.

In Glen Roy, Lochaber about 1885 the dancing was nearly always out of doors and at Bohenie, in the lower part of the Glen there is a flat topped hillock behind the house which is still known as Tom-na-Banais (the wedding knoll) from its use as the dancing place for weddings.

The curiously named dance, Bonny Briest Knots was always named as the first dance after the wedding supper when the bride and groom lead off the dance with the best man and the bridesmaid.

THE STEALING REEL

In Barra, the Stealing Reel, 'Ruidhleadh Ghoid' was last performed, although it was common all over the islands. This reel was the last one to take place before the ceremonial putting of the bride to bed. She and her bridegroom would be dancing this particular reel, when a couple of girls would sneak in, whisk her away and yet another lass would dance in her place.

Then the bridegroom would look around for his bride, and in a twinkling he too would be tweaked away by a couple of his friends and another young man would slide into his place. It was all done with as little disturbance to the dance as possible, indeed everyone would studiously ignore these goings on, for they were determined to ensure that with this event, the fairies would be cheated. A long-standing fear was that the fairies would steal the bride, hide her away and replace her with a magical figure, alluring but with a tendency to corrupt the groom.

Perhaps this stemmed from the Celtic mythological stories in which a witch disguised as a fairy would emerge from the loch, sea, or down from the mists and malevolently trick the bridegroom.

THE KISSING DANCE

On South Uist, in the last century, although even then it was dying out, the piper would play 'pog an toisach' kiss first before every dance. It was the last dance of the evening, at least as old as 1818, but dying out by the turn of the century.

According to a description of a Shetland wedding written in 1859 the custom was at that time observed at the end of each dance, but within living memory it took place only two or three times in an evening's dancing, generally at the end of the Shetland Reel.

A rather cross quote from an account of a Shetland wedding in 1837:

> 'Now the reel ends. Kiss the lasses, exclaims the lad with the hairy bonnet and four loud smacks are instantly heard, the lasses giving a twist or two in the arms of their partners, just for appearances sake,… this piece of hypocrisy is no fault of theirs but arises from the tyranny of fashion. Poor things, why should they not like a kiss as well as there other sex? and when we all know so well that they do, how absurd that fashion should force them to appear as if they didn't.'

RIGADOON-A-DAISY DANCE

Dancing outside clearly solved many problems of finding a convenient barn, and somewhere large enough to take all the assembled and invited company. These outdoor dances were charmingly named as 'rigadoon-a-daisy' dances.

> 'Lads an' lassies met at e'en
> An' danced the rigadoon-a-daisy,
> O'er the sinny simmer green.'

In Galloway around 1824,

> 'at weddings anciently the wadding fowk danced a great deal on the grass, before they went into the barns; this fun was termed rigadoon daisy.'

But the Lang Reel of Collieston appears to be the lengthiest, colourful most energetic and famous of all the wedding reels. Hearing the description of this event, some might wonder if the fishing folks vied with one another from village to village to see who could outdo the others in the sheer complexity and vivacity of their wedding dance.

The Lang Reel commenced after the ceremony and feast, attended by almost all members of the village. The wedding itself was full of fun and frivolity. Even the minister was required to enter into the spirit of the occasion. He would sport ribbons from his shoulders, and when once the local minister was unable to take the ceremony, a Reverend Ross of Cruden was asked to come over and deputise. So that he would be left in no doubt as to what was expected of him, blue ribbons were dispatched to the manse.

'He, then being an old man, rode proudly across to Collieston decked in his ribbons and most picturesque he looked on horseback.'

The reel has just been revived, and although not danced in this case after a wedding, its re-enactment as part of a village event gave ample excuse to a local dance enthusiast Lorna Maclaren to garner all available memories and information.

Her version of the dance commenced with the first man pulling out his handkerchief, placing it on the ground in front of his chosen lady, kneeling on it, then kissing her and asking her to dance, which meant setting to each other and spinning.

Then she chooses the next man, and they set and so on.

It appears that when originally danced, the whole company would eventually be waving their hankies, kissing chosen partners, and dancing, and then drop out again, until only the bride and groom were left.

Rear Admiral Steve Ritchie, who organised the modern day event in which the dance played a starring role, with the village company dancing down to the pier and on the sands on a glorious summers day, recalls his childhood in Collieston.

'When you pulled a hankie from your pocket, the old folk would say, 'Ye're awa to the Lang Reel nae doot'.'

THE SHAME REEL

The shame reel mainly appears to have been confined to fisher villages around the coast, as often the dance was performed on the sands.

'When me and Elspit was wed, we led off the shamit reel on the sands' is one account recorded in 1935 of a fisherman from somewhere around the East coast.

The curious name this reel acquired, 'shame spring', 'shame reel', 'shemit reel' appears to be so called because it was to 'take away the shame and bashfulness which the bride laboured under before so many people.'

Sometimes the reel was danced on the links or the sands, probably anywhere that was flattish and common ground. No doubt this was in the absence of a hall, or a room large enough to entertain all the guests, as in many villages the entire population would come to the celebration.

Generally, the shame reel was the first dance after the wedding. It was performed by the bride and the best man, and the bridegroom and the best maid (bridesmaid).

The bride's partner asked what music she would like, and she would traditionally reply, 'Through the warld will I gang wi' the lad that loes me', which seemed like an obvious choice. The fiddlers would then strike up, and the four dancers would dance this reel, to the silent audience of guests, who would wait until it was finished before applauding. After this ordeal, the atmosphere must have lightened, as the rest of the party then joined in. This account, from Forfarshire in 1880 notes that this dance 'was common in Forfarshire twenty years ago' and it appears that this traditional dance might have lost some of its colour by this time.

Back in 1823, a W.G. Stewart wrote that

'All the company assemble on the lawn with the flambeaux and form into a circle. The bridal pair and their retinue then dance a sixsome reel, each putting a piece of silver into the musician's hand.'

It is a tantalising description of a colourful and much performed wedding ritual. Sadly, though, the description of how exactly the reel was danced is totally lost.

THE SHAMEFUL REEL

The ancient church of Tullich, close to the A93, Aberdeen to Ballater road is surrounded by a circular wall, (no corners for the Devil to hide in) enclosing many ancient burial stones.

The name Tullich has its origins in the Gaelic 'tulach' meaning 'knoll'. The area is part of a larger area known as 'dalmuickeachie', or the 'field of the pigs', which is probably very pertinent. The area still supports a large forest of oak, the acorns from which wild pigs would have feasted upon.

Possibly in early times, the 'tulach' was a centre of pagan worship, but when St Nathalan, the great saint of Deeside arrived in the area, this became on of his centres of preaching, and the church took on his name until the Reformation in 1560 when it reverted to the original name, 'tulach', eventually becoming established as Tullich.

With such an important and chequered history it is odd that Tullich is remembered to this day through a dance. The Reel of Tullich is said to date from an incident when the congregation grew tired of waiting for the minister to turn up one obviously wintry morning. Some of the members of the congregation, so the story goes, started to stamp their feet to try and keep warm. One enterprising member of the crowd took himself off and returned with a keg of whisky from the local Inn, famous in its day, called the Stile o' Tullich. A fiddler struck up a tune and before long a full scale dance was taking place. The fun, of course was short-lived. The disapproving figure of the minister appeared to darken the doorway, taking in at a glance this sight of unseemly merriment within the church. His fury knew no limits. He cast upon his flock 'dool and destruction' to all who had partaken in this revelry and legend records that not a member of the dancing congregation was alive a year later.

Piecing together the evidence, this incident must surely have taken place after the Reformation. A hellfire and damnation minister freshly influenced by John Knox fits well into the tale. But believable?

The Reel of Tullich is alive and well to this day. Furthermore, it is danced in a straight line rather than a circle, as it would have been up and down the aisle – but the church sits now unroofed. Who indeed suffered as a result of the minister's fury?

WITH THANKS TO:

The many librarians, archivists and museum curators from all over Scotland who have patiently answered my questions as well as the exceptional tolerance of Jeremy Duncan of the Sandeman Library, Perth.

The National Trust for Scotland, and especially Mrs Margaret Cameron, the Education Advisor.

Historic Scotland, and especially Elspeth Henderson, Public Relations Officer.

Highland Heritage Museum at Kingussie.

The Scottish Ethnological Archive, Edinburgh.

Mr Steve Robertson and Mr Buff Hardie from *Scotland the What?* who allowed me to quote the irrepressible (but fictitious) Edinburgh Director of Town Planning from the book of their theatrical revues. *Scotland the What? Collected Sketches and Songs* was published in 1987 by Gordon Wright Publishing.

Rear Admiral Steve Ritchie of Collieston.

Mrs Sheena Archdale.

Captain Fairlie of Myres Castle.

Mr Nick Parsons of Polmaily House Hotel.

Councillor David Smith from Midlothian District Council.

Mr Stan Forrester of Kishorn.

Mr Havey Pitcher.

Mr John Duff of Braemar.

Index